# *NGOs and the Rural Poverty*

# *NGOs and the Rural Poverty*

*By*
**Dr. M. Lakshmi Narasaiah**
M.A., Ph.D.
*Professor of Economics,*
*Coordinator, Department of M.B.A.*
*Sri Krishnadevaraya University Post-graduate Centre,*
*Kurnool–518 002*
*Andhra Pradesh (India)*

**DISCOVERY PUBLISHING HOUSE**
**NEW DELHI**

First Published – 2005
Reprinted – 2017

ISBN: 978-81-7141-943-2



**NGOs and Rural Poverty**

*Published by:*
**DISCOVERY PUBLISHING HOUSE PVT. LTD.**
4383/4B, Ansari Road Darya Ganj
New Delhi - 110 002 (India)
Phone: +91-11-23279245, 43596064-65
Fax: +91-11-23253475
*E-mail:* discoverypublishinghouse@gmail.com
sales@discoverypublishinggroup.com
*web:* www.discoverypublishinggroup.com

*Printed at:*
Infinity Imaging Systems
Delhi

## Preface

Poverty has always been with us and for atleast forty years its alleviation has been the professed objective of many strategies to improve the lot of the Indians. But the way in which it has been conceived, however, has been subject to considerable change. Relatively little attention was paid to the development of the poor themselves. Rather, they were portrayed as among the beneficiaries of development in larger systems which were to provide the dynamic force for the elimination of poverty (from the "outside" as it were). Development was principally something that happened to the poor—on a "trickle-down" basis.

The simple assumption that the poor would benefit from general economic growth, without paying any special attention to them, changed somewhat in the late 1950s, when if was perceived that the poor might not automatically benefit from macro-economic development, but that they must benefit it the social stability needed for overall economic growth was to be assured. From this point there emerged a specific line of antipoverty thinking to improve the income of poor people.

The manner in which the poor were to be integrated into the overall growth process, however, was very specific. It was concerned not so much with what the poor could offer to the growth process—as with what they should receive from that process. For all its merits the Basic Needs strategy, and the social "safety net" approach which followed it, basically emphasized the consumption needs of the poor—and not their surplus producing possibilities. On the contrary, a persistent theme in the discourse about the economics of the poor has been the need for some sort of transfer of resources to them from more productive and dynamic sectors of accumulation. In short, the poor have been portrayed as a net burden on the growth process.

It is possible to introduce an element of differentiation into this picture: given that it is rarely alleged that low wages are an obstacle to accumulation and growth, the poor who have been characterized as a burden have tended to be those not directly integrated into nascent large-scale systems of production: these are the poor "peripheral" to modern economic process—a group which encompasses a large proportion of the urban population in India (principally employed in the "informal" sector), as well as a vast mass of small, but relatively independent agricultural producers. Implicitly, then, the concepts of "peripheral", small-scale and poor have been run together to form, in the realm of ideas, a more or less dependent mass. The number of people ostensibly in these categories is huge, and they seem to represent an enormous burden on development. They represent a development "problem", and an awesome one at that.

While substantial progress has been made in India in reducing the percentage of the rural population below nationally defined poverty line, the absolute number of the rural poor has increased. The growth of output did not bring about a significant improvement in the income share of the lowest nor an uniform reduction in the percentage of the rural population below the poverty line. The situation actually worsened. Less than half of the rural population in India has access to safe water or sanitation, and only 60 per cent had any access to health services. National data on life expectancy, infant mortality and literacy show improvements, but also the persistence of completely unacceptable conditions.

**Dr. M. Lakshmi Narasaiah**

# Contents

# 1 NGOs Better Than the State

Non-governmental organisations have become the new hope of development cooperation. Criticism of official and multilateral development assistance is mounting. After more than four decades of international cooperation, there is more poverty in the Third World (with the exception of a few countries) than ever before. It has become clear that existing instruments cannot bring about change. Even the large donor organisations doubt their own ability to solve problems and find their doubts confirmed by internal evaluations. What led to this state of affairs, and is there reason to hope that the NGOs can do a better job?

Development assistance started in 1949 with U.S. President Harry Truman's famous Point Four Programme (named after Point 4 of his inaugural speech in Congress on January 20, 1949) as a continuation of the Marshall Plan. The policy of containment of communism, which was originally restricted to Europe, thus became a global strategy. This origin was the reason that development assistance was geared from the beginning exclusively to governments, and not to social groups in the developing countries. The accusation that the U.S.A. as well as the other Western donors were willing to provide development assistance to any government, even the most under democratic and corrupt one, as long as it was an ally against communism, was never dropped.

Four decades later, when hardly anyone remembered the origins of this policy, the original goal was reached: Communism collapsed. In the interim, development assistance became independent: what was merely a means to an end for Truman in 1949 had became the goal itself: Liberation of all people not only from oppression, but also from hunger, want and desperation. However, it was now conceded, although hesitantly, that this particular goal had not been met: that in many countries a corrupt and dictatorial state class had been kept alive rather than development, and that democratisation had in fact been obstructed.

Simultaneously, an intensive discussion of two new themes began in intellectual circles in the U.S. The return of ethics in politics and a stronger influence of citizens in public affairs—against the background of governments which were no longer trusted to be able to solve social problems. Both themes have by now reached. Europe under the labels "Communitarianism" and "civil society" where they were taken up by the "new social movements." These include North-NGOs which are active in development cooperation and work with partner organisations in the south. It is important not to lose sight of this correlation with society's broader change of values.

The NGOs argue that they can circumvent the unwieldy bureaucratic planning and administration process; that they are flexible, efficient, close to the target groups, and democratic at the grassroots level, and that their funds flow directly to the poor. How accurate is this claim?

Little is known in the North about the NGOs of the South. The rural reconstruction movements, which exist in several Asian countries, date back to the twenties. Today, they are large organisations with hundreds or thousand of staff members. In India and Sri Lanka, groups try to realize the ideas of Mahatáma Gandhi. In Africa, self-help and solidarity groups at the village level have been a tradition for centuries. Ethnologists used to characterize them as "secret societies". The large organisations, which were established in Africa (later than in Asia) a few years ago, build on this tradition. In Latin America, an attempt is made to revive the models of cooperative work in the pre-columbian era.

It is a myth that these groups are egalitarian grassroots organisations. Those that actually function, at the village as well as at the regional or national level, do so thanks to the selfless involvement of individual persons, who are able to motivate others, come up with ideas, coordinate efforts, and bring about decisions. Social science has known since the studies of group dynamics and "democratic leadership" in the U.S. in the thirties that groups cannot be effective without such people. In the North they cannot work "directly with the poor" because this would presuppose that again we would be on location. The assistance depends on the cooperation of local organisations, which means their leaders. We tend to forget this too easily in our development jargon. The real chance for NGO leaders lies in the fact that they do not have to prevail against a rigid, bureaucratic apparatus, which tires to stop novel ideas just because they are new. On the other hand, this constellation also harbours the danger that imperiousness and autocratic structures will expand within the NGO sector just as at the state level. Who actually monitors the NGOs? Not just government ministers have been known to build their own private residences with development aid money. Some NGO executives are already guilty of doing the same.

# 2 NGOs: *Searching for Solid Ground*

The role of NGOs should be to foster the emergence of a world wide civil society, the first step towards making globalisation a more democratic affair. NGOs were not born yesterday, but the rising number of conflicts that have reverberated in recent decades around a world globalized in the neoliberal mould has led them to multiply and diversify into highly visible bodies.

Who are the main players in this process of globalisation? Governments (politics) and the market (the economy) are the twin pillars supporting the productive systems and structures of modern societies. So who has the legitimate right to change them? The societies themselves, for they alone are made up of citizens grouped together as a people, a nation or a country. The right does not belong to governments, state structures, corporate executives or markets. This is why, as NGOs, our attention is directed at civil society itself.

At the global level, our basic task is to foster the emergence of a worlwide civil society as a precondition to calling for a new style of globalisation: "world governance." Our mission is to encourage the refounding of globalisation along more democratic lines by taking part in public debate and promulgating the concept of world citizenship. The political stances we take and our lobbying activities, therefore, do not come out of the blue but are efforts to transmit the main currents and aspirations of public opinion and make this opinion stronger and clearer.

## The Tripartite Mirage

All NGO actions are based on an obvious priority, namely that of supporting social protests and public pressure during major negotiations taking place within the main circles of power. That is why the agreements we conclude and the alliances we forge are above all else aimed at organisations and movements arising from civil society. That is also why we build forums, coalitions and networks that straddle national borders. On the basis of our approach, we can think globally, set up links between the particular and the universal, swap experiences and keep ourselves regularly informed.

Today, global power is monopolized by major multilateral organisations, and is fundamentally anti-democratic in its structure and working. In their current form, these organisations' claims to embody democracy and universal citizenship ring hollow. In fact, their only possible claim to legitimacy is through the vote. But not all the national governments represented in international organisations have been elected by popular suffrage, and very few of them represent all the different social forces that go into making up their nations.

Does this mean that NGOs, which are supposed to embody civil society, should claim to represent these people? Does it mean that our goal should be to win a place at the heart of a future new world democratic order? Does it mean that we are fully entitled to a seat in some new tripartite structure-made up of government, companies and civil society-that some people are campaigning for? In my opinion, all of that is just a mirage; even worse, we risk losing sight of our most useful and most legitimate purpose if we embrace that vision.

## Small Players, Big Issues

NGOs are not out to conquer power or win elections, be they world, national or local bodies. We are not set up like political parties, even though our activities are public and seem highly politicized. We cannot even present ourselves as representatives of civil society because civil society has not entrusted us with any such mandate.

So what do we want? To reach out, mobilized, educate, get across messages, suggest, innovate, persuade and politically strengthen various groups in civil society and, more specifically, those excluded from the decision making process. We want to give a voice to ideas, values, questions and proposals that involve social justice, a more equitable distribution of wealth, respect for the environment, the struggle against poverty and social exclusion.

Who are we? Small players, compared to the other pillars of civil society, such as trade unions and professional organisations, or bodies in the state or the market. But we are also—and this is something new—"big" players, because our mission and our field of action are not limited to a given society, national economy or single government. Our task is to form a bridge between the local and the global: in other words, to deal with what is universal, with what is common to all humanity. Human rights, social crises and environmental protection are global issues. We deal with them in specific situations, but our perspective is always planetary.

So where does our legitimacy lie? In the quality of the values, principles and ideals we defend. In the relevance and the importance of the issues we raise. In the inventiveness of the proposals we put forward. Our only source of legitimacy is our ability to develop ideas aimed at action—ideas that are up to the standards of public duty to which we aspire.

# 3 No Miracle Weapon for Development: *The Challenges Facing NGOs in the 21st Century*

Not only official development policy, but also the work of NGOs has come under pressure to reform. The optimistic belief that cooperation with NGO partners in the South would lead quasi automatically to better results has faded. In this sector, too, questions are being asked about efficiency control, better coordination, and focus instead of a 'shotgun' approach to the work.

In the case of NGOs engaged in development policy, it is not only their standing that has become greater. Their number, budgets and influence—and their closeness to governments—have also gained in quantity and strength. NGOs are now 'in' with governments, the media and international development cooperation agencies. NGOs are seen as the 'miracle weapon' in the battle against increasing poverty in large parts of the world.

The NGOs closeness to grassroots organisations in the South, their emphasis on help for self-help, and their independence from the foreign policy and economic interests of the North, allows them to orient their cooperation activities on the basic needs of the people in developing countries. And that enables the NGOs to make a credible and effective contribution to social change. But this self-made claim leads the public to expect big things of the organisations, which perhaps cannot be fulfilled.

The NGOs have largely failed to address this point, thereby missing the opportunity to take a self-critical look at themselves. Only such a stock taking, however, would permit answers to the question of what the NGOs will stand for in the 21st century.

To claim that we could give the answer in this article would be presumptuous. But we would like to outline three challenges which, we believe, the NGOs should in future tackle more robustly. In doing so, we shall concentrate on North NGOs and their branches in the developing countries.

## Focus on Core Tasks

NGOs are increasingly assuming tasks, which earlier were the domain of government actors. For example, the organisations support, among the things, the expansion of infrastructure in urban as well as rural areas, and public health and education systems. Various factors are helping to drive this development.

First, the neo-liberal concepts of many structural adjustment programmes have made developing country governments pull out of political areas which in most industrialised nations are controlled by governments, if not implemented by them.

Second, donor governments are happy to give up cooperating with inefficient and sometimes intractable official partner structures if NGOs offer themselves as competent intermediaries or implementing organisations.

Third, the industrialised nations' development cooperation agencies score a double coup by such switching of responsibility for a project. They gain vicarious kudos from the NGO's positive image, and moreover can be pretty sure that the NGO side will not criticise the measures.

Finally, in line with the liberal ethos on democracy, the NGOs are regarded as the champions of democratisation and the foundation of a civil society.

This leads to the NGOs running the risk of obligingly allowing themselves to be instrumentalised as the fill-in for the cut backs and failure of official development cooperation and becoming the victims of their own claims. To date, nothing has indicated that, measured against developmental benchmarks such as effectiveness, efficiency and significance, the quality of NGO inputs in such sectors as infrastructure and advisory services for parastatals is better than that of government implementation organisations.

An undisputed strength of the North NGOs is that they have good contacts with their local counterparts of self-help initiatives, and many years' experience in this sector. But being close to the grassroots reduces the financial volume of potential intervention because that depends to great degrees on the limited capacity of the partner on site to absorb large sums of money. Moreover, North NGOs are as a rule too small and too diversified to achieve the degree of specialisation necessary for professional assessment and supervision of promotional measures. Not least, the NGO's target groups want mostly a package of measures more akin to community development approaches than to single sector projects.

These strengths and weaknesses present guidelines for defining the NGOs' core tasks. They should focus on their strengths to give their profile sharper edges. That includes pointing out to the industrialised nations development cooperation agencies their own core missions. Instead of perfoming in non-government sectors, to which its instruments are not suited, official development cooperation should, rather, ensure that developing country governments and their administrative bodies can competently fulfill their tasks.

## Cooperation Instead of Competition

Whoever travels through developing countries today, sees at many crossroads signs that point in al directions to the locations of local NGOs. Not all NGOs are competent, not all are grassroots-orientated, and not a few are simply labels for private business sector initiatives or the sinecures of representatives of the state elite. Neither representatives of North NGOs nor government implementing orgaisations find it easy to separate the wheat from the chaff. But in only a few (praiseworthy) cases is there an exchange of information among the international actors, apparently because every organisation wants to shield its local partners from the others.

The had led on the one hand to the South NGOs also having long played the game known in official development cooperation circles as 'donor rotation'. As soon as one donor completes a project, another steps into replace him. Interventions also are too often not harmonised.

This criticism does not mean there should be no competition to find the best solution to a problem. On the contrary, specific processes should be made transparent and discussed so that one can differentiate between reports of short-lived success and approaches aligned on the long haul. Indeed, perhaps that would enable learning from others and lead to good ideas being taken up by several. Many North NGOs appear not even to have a need for reciprocal information flows and case-to-case harmonisation, which are gradually gaining a foothold in official development cooperation—although with many setbacks due to well-known national interests.

So long as there is no government framework for their activities, NGOs should strengthen their attempts to harmonise their support measures with other actors. This does not contradict NGO enterprise. An unfortunately frequent deficit of developing countries is that their governments do not define scope for developmental action. This means that both official and non-governmental development cooperation operate in a political vacuum which gives every well-meaning dilettante room for experiments.

NGOs can be proud of their contribution to the consolidation of human rights in many societies, and of their efforts for civil rights and for more efficient local organisations with a greater capability to handle conflicts. NGOs also have won great credit by pointing out to government actors deficiencies and weak spots in developmental practice. Without the NGOs' pressure and that of their lobby, the cross-sectorial topics of the environment, women and poverty—which are now firmly fixed in development cooperation—would not have entered the international political debate so quickly nor have been implemented in projects and programmes.

NGOs would be well advised to get together as soon as possible to define and agree on criteria for the quality of their work. They should also carry out evaluations that identify and clearly describe the impacts of their efforts.

The basis of the evaluations should be a joint code or common denominator for the most important developmental benchmarks, such as sustainability and subsidiary. This would be right for the peculiarities of the many NGOs, and not result in all organisations being lumped together.

## Power or Importence Instrumentalised

NGOs are not the 'miracle weapon' they have allowed themselves to be labelled. Their positive image has so far been enough to retain the goodwill of members of the public who are interested in developmental matters, especially that of donors. But that can change quickly if the NGOs allow themselves to be instrumentalised by their own governments, if government organisations overtake them in efficiency control, and if they cannot convincingly present their core tasks for the present and future. That applies above all if they criticise others without putting their own house in order. An also if they aim to steal silently away from goals such as solidarity, social change and innovation.

It is not about random concepts, but central challenges. NGOs that want to do more than just survive but aim at effective, high-quality and professional work targeted on social change in partner countries should confront these challenges aggressively. Otherwise, the "Power of the Courageous" will one day turn into the importance of those who came too late.

# 4 Who is Responsible for Corruption in Aid?

World Bank President James Wolfensohn's pronouncement that the 'cancer' of corruption seriously undermines development and will not be tolerated in future Bank funded projects, prompts one to ask: where and when did this corruption originate? How much corruption is acceptable to the World Bank and donor community? For many years the World Bank tended to ignore or discount the significance of corruption in its operations. Donor agencies in general seem to have a very high tolerance for the misuse of their money. Now that the Bank, the UK system, and bilateral agencies are under growing pressure to improve their performance, they are seeking ways to limit the corrupt use of aid money. For the moment, there is little or no evidence that they have any idea of how to go about the task.

One of the main reasons for the disappointing performance of structural adjustment programmes is the misuse of donor money, including systematic corruption. An extreme example is Tanzania's import support programme, which allowed local manufacturers and traders to import raw materials and finished goods. An increasing number of companies, both private and parastatal, began to abuse the system. They stopped paying counterpart funds. Import duty and sales tax were not paid on imports. Neither the Treasury nor the commercial banks had the administrative capacity or the integrity to handle large volumes of free foreign exchanges, but the donors ignored the problem. Only when the scandalous behaviour of the banks, the Treasury and the Minister of Finance had reached epic proportions, fuelling inflation and completely derailing the budgetary process, did the World Bank and other donors finally pull the plug on import support.

In December 1996, the IMF started disbursing US$240 million enhanced structural adjustment loan, but to date not one private or parastatal company has been put in receivership for the hundreds of millions of donor dollars which went astray via import support. This casual approach to large-scale corruption has been the norm among donors.

Some bilateral donors have cut the number of countries which they assist, and eradicated funds to those remaining. To increase aid effectiveness some of them also reduced the number of sectors they support per country. Add to this the tendency for the whole donor community to move into new activities at the same time, and you have a recipe for too much aid chasing too little 'absorptive capacity' in the countries of concentration, which include Tanzania, Uganda and Kenya, Pressure to spend has led to unbelievable over-funding in certain sectors. Well-known examples are NGOs, many of which are created with the sole objective of embezzling donor money.

With the coming of political pluralism, a growing volume of aid money has been channeled into 'governance' activities. The disadvantages of governance from the donor perspective are that donors have little experience in this field, and the amounts of money, which can be disbursed, compared to the amount of administrative work involved, are relatively trivial.

Aid has served to encourage the establishment of a whole range of corrupt activities in 'civil society' to add to those which already existed in the state apparatus. Many of those managing the corruption are recent migrants from the state sector, or straddle both public and private sectors. The politically acceptable employment of more local personnel as desk officers has served to increase the rate of corruption. The chances of being caught or punished are minimal. The few genuine local change-agents are crowded out by the charlatans and opportunists. The imperative to disburse at all costs makes it very difficult for donors to adequately monitor or evaluate the quality of their assistance, since it would put the agencies in a poor light if they were seen to be supporting non-performning and corrupt activities. Thus, as has generally been the case, the donors pretend that their assistance is being well used, and are even prepared to deny well-founded allegations of the misuse of project funds.

The new aid activities discussed above account for a relatively small proportion of total aid flows, however. The basic issue is the amount of uncontrolled corruption which still characterizes the World Bank and other donors' more traditional project, programme, and financial support. Here too one finds projects of ever growing magnitude, as the big spending goes on. The continued availability of donor money is the major determinant of the volume of aid, not performance, structural reform, or impact on 'target groups'. Although further project aid cannot be justified on the basis of past performance, it continues to be a major form of aid delivery by both the World Bank and other donor agencies.

The picture which emerges is that of an oppressed people largely at the mercy of an incompetent and corrupt state apparatus. The role of aid in helping to create and reproduce this lamentable state of affairs is worth exploring. Unfortunately, the report does not mention corruption in aid. If corruption has become one of the major international issues of modern times, it would hardly be surprising to find that the virus has already infected and is spreading within the major agencies.

If countries with as much corruption as Tanzania, Uganda, and Kenya can continue to enjoy billions of dollars of aid every year, it is not because they have demonstrated their ability to use aid wisely. But the donors are not well placed to extol the virtues of transparency and accountability which they do not practice themselves. To address the question of corruption in aid, the World Bank and other agencies will have to take a along look at their own role in creating the problem which they now propose to cure.

# 5 The Dynamics of Rural Poverty in India

Poverty is homogeneous only when considered from the point of view of income or consumption: the uniformity of the poor as a category exists only on the level of the fact that they have little to consume. When considered from the point of view of production, i.e., the circumstances in which the poor must operate to gain their income, the conditions of poverty are extraordinary diverse. A concrete grasp of these diverse circumstances is the first step in developing relevant instruments to address not only the problems of the poor, but also the challenge of taking advantage of the opportunities available to them.

The conventional means of measuring economic progress, such as Gross National Product per cpita, tell us little about the real nature of poverty. In recent years this sort of yardstick has been supplemented by measurements of food security, income distribution, and social development (encompassing health and education). These offer the possibility of composite indices, allowing the development of more rounded characterisations and comparisons of poverty at the national level. However, these principally refer to the symptoms of poverty, not to the relational factors generating it. Poverty is not a state of being, it is the effect of dynamic processes. While it is important to know where poverty is greatest, it is critical to know why it exists. This inquiry necessarily leads away from the nature of the poor as individuals to the nature of their social and physical environment. Poverty is not only a personal phenomenon, it is a social status. As such, while its effects can be measured on the level of the individual, its causes must be sought elsewhere. From the point of view of poverty alleviation the process of becoming is just as important as the state of being.

At the heart of poverty is the inadequate access of the poor to productive resources. Low incomes tend to reflect inadequate means of production, not incompetent producers. However, poverty in India is not simply a reflection of private resources. A broad range of "external" factors impinge on incomes, among them the following:

## National Policies

One of the ironies of Indian development is that while no government wants poverty, many policies contribute to it—what is given in anti-poverty programmes is drained away by other policies. The poor do not always come out ahead in the balance—they are often net "donors" to the rest of society. Frequent reference is made to unsustainable forms of development—to urban over-expansion, industrialisation based on subsidies, and to public sector engorgement. What is less frequently realized is that the bill for these phenomena is often presented to the rural poor. Taxation of exports to sustain sectors with little export potential of their own and subsidized food imports to supply the urban population are policies that are often paid for by the rural poor. In many areas of India, exports are agricultural goods produced by small farmers. Here export taxes contribute to rural poverty. The same is true of "cheap" food imports which depress the prices paid to small farmers for their food crops.

"Structural imbalance" is not only a recipe for increasing external indebtedness, it is also a recipe for increasing the poverty of the rural population. The political weakness of the poor in most areas is not only the basis for inadequate poverty alleviation programmes and policies—it is the basis for an actual transfer of their income to more socially influential groups. While it is often correctly asserted that the poor are the first to suffer from adjustments involving public social expenditure cuts, it is often the case that they also have the most to gain from the elimination of policy-based economic distortions that reflect social power rather than productive efficiency and potential.

## Demographic Factors

Accelerated population growth is a long-term contributor to poverty. In India the incomes of the poor have declined, mortality rates are also falling, pushing the numbers up. In the meantime, land is becoming scarcer, plots more fragmented and the soil and pasture increasingly degraded. This phenomenon is not without its policy dimensions. As long as the poor remain undercapitalized, and essential determinant of household income is the amount of labour available to its household economic strategies favour large families. While population policy has a role to play, possibly more critical is a change in the economic environment. Access to capital and more secure income changes perceptions of the need for labour. In the medium and long-term, population dynamics are driven by the underlying productive systems. As long as the production systems of the poor remain underdeveloped, population growth remains high, restricting even the future possibility of development.

## Natural Resource Management and the Environment

If poverty is both cause and effect of rapid population expansion, so poverty is both cause and effect of many dimensions of degradation of the environment. Many of the rural poor, but by no means all, live in areas of extreme environmental fragility, a circumstance often prompted by high level of control by the better-off over more stable and productive resource areas. Here the poor are extraordinarily exposed to the dangers of erosion, whittling away at an already meager productive base. The threat is not entirely due to nature. Rather, poverty accelerates erosion. Without capital, the poor are frequently unable to invest in even traditional methods of soil and water conservation. And without sufficient land they are forced to shorten fallow periods, putting further strain on the resource base. As in the case of population growth, the result is strain not only on the poor, but on the entire Indian economy. Given the extremely limited economic alternatives, the solution to this problem is not to forbid the use of environmentally fragile resources to the poor, it is to change the conditions under which their use takes place. Access to conservation technology is important; but more so are security of land tenure and resources to invest.

Combating poverty means not only increasing the production of the poor, but also preserving and enhancing the long-term value of the resource they control. What this very often means, in practice is assisting the poor in reestablishing a stable relationship with fragile resource. Prevailing processes in many areas involve the gradual—and sometimes not so gradual—depletion of natural resources, to the detriment of all. Part of the answer to this is conservation. Part of the answer is also to provide viable economic alternatives to the poor, reducing their dependence on erosion-prone crop and livestock practices.

### Exploitative Intermediates

The poor are not unaware of the pressure upon them, and also of means of overcoming them. Their ability to respond, however, is severely impaired by social powerlessness. The poor are surrounded by a dense network of public and private factors reducing their freedom of action, and actually draining what few resources they do have. Members of the network include traders and moneylenders capitalizing upon the economic weakness of the poor, and engaging them in unequal exchanges. They also include public agencies either indifferent to the requirements of the socially uninfluential, or actively engaged in extracting "surplus" for use by other groups. Not to be excluded from this are organisations which are ostensibly "for" the poor, but which, in fact, serve as systems of containment and control.

# 6 Overcoming the Poverty in India and the Lessons Learned

Basic elements in the struggle against poverty in India are the provision of the economic services and assets which the poor have tended not to receive in the past—as a result of oversight or design. The emphasis on economic services and assets is just because the mass of the rural poor are self-employed, and it is upon the improvement in the means of production directly accessible to them that their prosperity depends. Health and education are very important, but offer more if combined with the material means of making a living—of putting body and mind to work. These assets and services include land, water, technology, commercial services, handling output and inputs, and credit—provided within an economic policy famework conductive to their optimal exploitation.

This list is hardly new. It corresponds to the requirements of any producer. The basic points to be made in this regard are: firstly, that the general requirements of poor producers are precisely the same as those of other producers and that measures to alleviate poverty that fall short of recognizing the full range of such requirements are doomed to failure; and, secondly, that these assets and services are not typically provided in a form accessible to the poor. India has made important progress in providing a more effective framework for agricultural production "in general", this framework has not properly embraced small and poor producers. They are as follows:

## Access to Land and Water

In the case of access to land, for example, land reform efforts in India has frequently involved major loop-holes, allowing the socially powerful to minimize *de facto* improvements in the condition of the poor. In the critical area of land rights, registration processes have been so complex and costly relative to the resources of the poor that land regularization programmes have, sometimes unintentionally, become virtual characters for legalizing the eviction of the poor and the actual loss of their traditional rights. Irrigation without specific measures to defend the interests of existing occupants of area exposes them to expulsion—and, moreover, has tended to be concentrated in large-scale schemes benefiting already high potential areas in which the better-off predominate. While huge sums have been spent on large-scale irrigation schemes, little has been spent on water conservation and the sort of small-scale developments that are more likely to be of relevance to marginal small-scale producers.

## Technology Transfer

In the area of technology, attention has been focused on technologies (such as the Green Revolution) requiring extensive access to water and, fertilizers, neither of which are generally available among the poor. In fact, research almost every-where has concentrated on larger-scale production in areas of relatively high resource endowment. In contrast to this, research relevant to small-scale producers in marginal soil and rainfed areas in India has been shockingly deficient. As in other fields, this is partly explicable in terms of a frequently unproved belief that large-scale production is more efficient. It is also explicable in terms of the fact that it is the powerful who set the research agenda, not the poor. Taking its inspiration from highly specialized, large-scale agricultural units of production, research has tended to dwell separately on individual crops—rather than on the interaction between crops, which is of much greater relevance to small-scale producers engaging in highly complex systems of production to maximize food self-sufficiency and minimize risks.

## Commercial Services

In the area of handling of output and inputs, organized services (not infrequently under public control in the past) have tended to concentrate in the proximity of large-scale producers and users of input in relatively well-endowed areas. In India the poor have had to incur the extraordinary costs of handling their own transport of goods to and from service points—frequently over long and deficient lines of communication. The alternative has been to resort to private intermediaries offering goods, and buying products, at prices very different from those enjoyed by larger producers. In effect, the better-off and the poor have confronted different sets of prices—with the poor paying more for what they buy, and receiving less for what they sell.

## Credit

In the area of credit, the situation has been disastrous. It is generally recognised that productive improvement needs a change in means of production—new tools, improved seeds, fertilizers, etc. Such a change everywhere is typically effected on the basis of credit. Yet rural credit schemes in India have usually not extended support to small farmers and the poor. Credit has been concentrated among richer farmers with collateral and with demand for larger loans. In order to improve their productivity, the poor have been forced to seek credit from informal money-lenders-at virtually confiscatory rates. Again, the cost of modernization has been much higher for the poor than for the better-off. The inevitable result has been a lower rate of change, and the consolidation, rather than the reduction of poverty.

## The Victims Blamed

Although vast amounts of money have been invested in rural development in India, very little of it has reached the poor. The poor have been left to their own devices, while the better-off have received a wide range of assistance—not infrequently allowing them to encroach further upon the land of the poor. Support for agricultural expansion has not led to rural development, and it has not eliminated rural poverty. The relatively undynamic performance of many small-scale farmers under these circumstances is frequently taken as "proof" that they are a poor investment. This is a variant of "blaming the victim". In fact, the poor have fared badly, not because they could not efficiently use support, but because they did not get it.

In other words, the failure of the poor to benefit from agricultural sector investments has not reflected an economic failure among the poor themselves. Rather, it has involved policy and institutional failures. On the policy level, it has tended to reflect an unwillingness to restrain the socially influential from seeking to monopolize scarce resources to their own benefit—and, perhaps, a lack of awareness of the incompatibility between apparently "natural" criteria for support (e.g., the demand for land title as collateral for credit) and the particular circumstance of poor and small farmers (e.g., involvement) in traditional forms of land tenure). On the institutional level, it has involved both unwillingness to give weight to the requirements of the poor, and lack of initiative in solving real problems in providing services to the poor such as the high cost of providing services on an individual basis to a large number of small and often dispersed "clients". While there has been a great deal of lamentation about poverty in India, remarkably little has been done to change it at the level of economic systems—perhaps because social welfare activities are much easier to implement than real policy and institutional changes. It is possible to do very much better—not by simply pouring in more resources (in channels which at times do not even ultimately reach the poor), but by changing the framework of investment, i.e., the instruments of development.

## LESSONS LEARNED

### Targeting of Resources

The fundamental lessons learned are that investment resources must be targeted at the poor. In a world of competition for scarce resources, investments in rural development tend to be captured by those with national and local power—a group, which rarely encompasses the rural poor. The first step in delivering resources to the poor is establishing strict criteria for eligibility for assistance. Indicators of wealth in India vary according to the nature of the local economy—in some cases it is extent of land ownership, in others size of cattle herds, in yet others ownership of draught animals—but the principle remains the same: investment in those with the least assets. In some cases, for example, where women represent a significant proportion of actual producers, this may give rise to entirely new patterns of investment.

### Reorienting Institutions

The intention to distribute resources to the poorest is not always accompanied by actual performance. Among the reasons for this is the inappropriateness of delivery mechanisms. Put simply, institutions long oriented to the non-poor have tended to develop operating procedures and structures which reflect the nature of their de facto clientele and which hinder them from serving a new target group. In the area of credit, for example, insistence upon collateral in land may be an absolute obstacle to participation by the poor—just as a limited banking network may represent an obstacle to delivery to the poor, for whom the costs of communicating with a bank at considerable distance might well add significantly to the real cost of credit. Effectively channeling resources to the poor, therefore, means the elaboration of institutional means of delivery consistent with their circumstances.

However, it must be recognized that there are exceptional institutional costs associated with providing services to (and among) the poor—costs arising from the fact that there are many individuals involved, and that their individual requirement tend to be quite small. The costs of government services in, for example, agricultural credit, are necessarily higher if this involves a very large number of small producers than if it involves a small number of large producers. Administration costs in banking tend to be much higher relative to loan volume if it involves a myriad of individual small loans. These factors have often been adduced as reasons for the "impossibility" of serving the poor. Effective Service appears financially impossible, especially the context of widespread retrenchment in public expenditure under structural adjustment programmes. The poor are often willing to pay the actual costs of services—especially if the alternative is no service at all, or supply by local informal monopolists. On the other hand, there are proven ways of reducing costs of service supply to the poor—by involving the poor themselves. Everywhere in India poor people overcome some of the obstacles involved in their individual poverty through cooperation and joint action. While such organization typically develops in the absence of formal service organizations and markets, it can also develop in association with formal organizations. In effect, the organized small farmer can help shoulder the cost of services through organizing local level distribution and administration themselves.

## People's Participation

People's participation is, therefore, not only a "social" concept. It is an eminently economic concept, involving cost sharing. It is fundamental to the sustainability of improvements. The long-term solution is not to throw money at the problems of the poor, but to help them to organize to overcome themselves. One of the happy externalities of this approach is not only lower cost services, but services more likely to be in harmony with what small farmers perceive themselves as needing.

## Balanced Development

Development means change, not only in the volume of production, but in the composition of output and the conditions under which it is produced. What is argued is that the pursuit of development without the inclusion of the mass of small-scale producers and the poor has important structural drawbacks, and that their inclusion offers the basis for more sustainable long-term development. Some smallholder groups have a vast unutilized potential for expansion. Others have much more modest prospects.

Even those with the poorest assets and possibilities however, can be helped to improve their condition. While the direct economic benefits of this may be relatively slender, the side-effects may be great. An eventual shift of these groups to other areas and systems of production might be inevitable if aspirations for a better life are to be satisfied, but it is essential that this shift be orderly necessitating that support be given in the transitional period. This support can be either a direct welfare transfer or an investment in productive capacity. In many cases the latter may be the least-cost alternative.

The issue, then, is neither the "rich way" nor the "poor way". What is required is: an unprejudiced evaluation of the capacities and possibilities of poor and small-scale producers, and their potential role in the overall scheme of national development; allocation of investment resources according to potential and within an institutional framework ensuring delivery and profitable use; and a more balanced view of the overall social costs and benefits of alternative means of addressing transitional states. The belief is that the outcome of this will involve a reappraisal of the role of the poor in economic development, and a major improvement in the state of the rural poor throughout India.

The poor are many, their productive potential is great, but in few places is the exploitation of this potential an explicit focus of policy concern and action—although everywhere it is the concern of the poor themselves. While concrete evidence of the efficacy of systematic policy of support to the poor is sparse (simply because it has so rarely been tried), the evidence of its effectiveness on the local level is abundant.

# 7 Rural Poverty in India

"It is morning in a remote farming area in India. As her husband harnesses a bullock to plough their field, a woman pounds the grain she will use for the day's main meal. Three kilometres away, their children are collecting fuelwood and water before starting their morning walk to school".

"After school, they help their mother light a fire with a few sticks, milk the cow and collect the sundried grain. That evening, as the family rests around the hearth, father worries about how to sell his onions before they spoil and the price falls. Before sleeping his wife prepares a basket of home-grown vegetables to sell next day at the village market five kilometres away. With the takings, she hopes to buy a kerosene lamp although she might not have enough cash left to buy the kerosene immediately...."

That description of rural life is a daily reality for hundreds of millions of families throughout India. Rural poverty, 1990s means subsistence on the meagre earnings of wage labour or unreliable harvests from small plots of land. It means raising a family without safe drinking water or proper sanitation, suffering disease or injury without medical assistance. In times of unemployment or crop failure, it means living with the pangs of hunger—and the risk of death by famine.

## Inside the Poverty Trap

Poverty in rural India is created and perpetuated by a number of closely interlinked socio-economic processes:

1. Policies and institutional arrangements biased against the poor exclude them from the benefits of

development, frustrate their productive potential and accentuate the impact of other poverty processes.

Institutional processes that perpetuate rural poverty include lack of access to land, inequitable share-cropping and tenancy arrangements, poor markets, limited access to credit, inputs and technology, and ineffective extension services. Other constraints are lack of training facilities, inadequate research related to smallholder farming systems, and last but not least a lack of grassroots institutions needed to foster people's participation.

Policy and institutional biases have short and long-term impacts. In the short term, the poor are unable to earn enough to meet nutritional requirements or to take advantage of the market. "In the longer term", "poor households continue to lag behind because they do not generate a surplus for investment, nor do they have access to investment opportunities. Moreover, the rural poor may be forced to overuse resources, which undermines productivity and income".

2. Even today dualistic agrarian structures originating in colonial times persist. In India, highly capitalized large and medium-sized farms have virtually monopolistic control over land and labour at the expense of the small farm sector. Large scale commercial producers—control the best farm land. Resources have been funnelled into irrigated plantations producing cotton and mechanized cultivation of sorghum. In marginal areas, mechanisation has led to environmental degradation and the loss of seasonal grazing and stock routes for pastoralists.

"Thus, side by side with modern agriculture, millions of marginal farmers and herdsmen subsist far below the poverty line". This dualism severely limits their capacity to grow food and accumulate capital. They lack marketable surpluses, and incentives and opportunities to save and invest.

3. Rapid population growth can cause and perpetuate rural poverty by increasing pressure on limited productive resources, social services and employment, as well as paradoxically—creating labour shortages through outmigration.

   The most obvious consequence of rapid population growth is that, even with relatively high rates of economic growth, improvements in living conditions are limited. Total saving in the economy declines, leaving fewer resources for investment in human development. Negative consequences are most acute in rural areas. Growing population often combined with traditional laws of inheritance—has led to fragmentation of holdings, degradation of crop and pasture land, and falling yields. In areas with unequal distribution of land, rapid population growth has accelerated proletarisation of the rural work force and reduced incomes.

4. Rural poverty, malnutrition and undernutrition are closely linked to environmental degradation. Poor people in marginal areas are destroying natural resources as they struggle to keep their production systems sustainable. In acute shortage of arable land has forced farmers to reduce the length of fallow periods and plough up land previously reserved for grazing. These practices have led to declining yields, soil depletion and further impoverishment. Population pressure is pushing weaker members of the rural community into ecologically vulnerable areas.

   Degradation of the environment is strongly linked to household food insecurity and lack of fuel. Much of the fragile forest cover has been destroyed by poor rural people in the search for grazing land and fuel wood.

   Government policies have also wrought environmental damage. A rapid expansion of areas under crops often accelerates deforestation and land degradation.

Programmes to expand cereal production into marginal areas, subsidized capital to support commercial operations subsidies for inappropriate technologies and excessive transfer of income out of the agricultural sector may undermine the sustainability of smallholders and pastoralists' production systems.

Inadequate public investment in off-farm employment and infrastructure, a lack of price incentives and inadequate access to modern agricultural inputs and services discourage investment in land conservation, leading to further overuse and degradation.

5. As poverty undermines traditional social bonds, the marginalisation of women has become a fact of rural life in India. With little or no access to land, millions of women depend on casual employment on meagre wages. Often, they farm fragmented plots of poor quality. Limited access to inputs, extension, training and credit limits, in turn, their ability to enter commercial agriculture.

   The exodus of males in search of work in urban areas (itself an indicator of poverty) has serious consequences for the women they leave behind. Output from land often falls and less attention is paid to maintenance, setting the stage for a long-term decline in productivity. Many female headed households have abandoned the use of oxen for ploughing, some plough and plan late and others no longer weed their fields.

6. The ethnic or cultural marginalisation of tribal or minority populations also plays a role in poverty. Many of these groups are further threatened by newly marginalized groups as the expansion of cultivation reduces and grazing areas of nomadic herders.

7. Exploitative middlemen also perpetuate rural poverty. Landlords exploit share croppers and tenants, moneylenders exploit debtors, and traders exploit small scale producers. During seasonal food shortages, the

poor may have to borrow money at interests rates exceeding 20 per cent a month. Force to devote most of their energies to debt servicing, they sink deeper into the poverty trap.

In some cases, government controlled co-operatives and government agencies whose task is to protect the poor may themselves practise forms of exploitation. Heavy levies imposed by government agencies have damaged small farmers. Large, inefficient bureaucracies are paid for by the productive sectors of the community and frequently contribute to the accumulation of large budget deficits.

8. Political troubles and civil strife have had a disastrous impact on the rural poor, one effect is the disruption of development assistance to the rural poor, both from national and international agencies. Another is the transformation of many producers into consumers of social services with serious consequences for production, savings, capital accumulation and investment.

9. The international economic environment directly influences the well-being of the Indian poor. Falling commodity prices and protectionist policies in India affect the employment and incomes of plantation workers and smallholders producing for export, particularly those relying heavily on a few agricultural commodities. Changes in international interest rates have repeatedly hurt smallscale producers in debt-burdened India, While world grain price increases has triggered rural famines.

The net flow of development resources to agriculture also affects rural poverty. Official development funding for food and agriculture increased between 1975 and 1982, but has fluctuated irregularly since. Moreover, concern with trade balances is diverting resources to export crops, sometimes at the expense of traditional crops grown by poor farmers.

# 8 The Persistence of Indian Poverty and its Alleviation

Poverty has always been with us and for at least forty years its alleviation has been the professed objective of many strategies to improve the lot of the Indians. But the way in which it has been conceived, however, has been subject to considerable change. Relatively little attention was paid to the development of the poor themselves. Rather, they were portrayed as among the beneficiaries of development in larger systems which were to provide the dynamic force for the elimination of poverty (from the "outside" as it were). Development was principally something that happened to the poor—on a "trickle-down" basis.

The simple assumption that the poor would benefit from general economic growth, without paying any special attention to them, changed somewhat in the late 1950s, when it was perceived that the poor might not automatically benefit from macro-economic development, but that they must benefit if the social stability needed for overall economic growth was to be assured. From this point there emerged a specific line of antipoverty thinking to improve the income of poor people.

The manner in which the poor were to be integrated into the overall growth process, however, was very specific. It was concerned not so much with what the poor could offer to the growth process—as with what they should receive from that process. For all its merits the Basic Needs strategy, and the social "safety net" approach which followed it, basically emphasized the consumption needs of the poor—and not their surplus producing possibilities. On the contrary, a persistent theme in the discourse about the economics of the poor has been the need for some sort of transfer of resources to them from more productive and dynamic sectors of accumulation. In short, the poor have been portrayed as a net burden on the growth process.

It is possible to introduce an element of differentiation into this picture: given that it is rarely alleged that low wages are an obstacle to accumulation and growth, the poor who have been characterized as a burden have tended to be those not directly integrated into nascent large-scale systems of production: these are the poor "peripheral" to modern economic process—a group which encompasses a large proportion of the urban population in India (principally employed in the "informal" sector), as well as a vast mass of small, but relatively independent agricultural producers.

Implicitly, then, the concepts of "peripheral", small-scale and poor have been run together to form, in the realm of ideas, a more or less dependent mass. The number of people ostensibly in these categories is huge, and they seem to represent an enormous burden on development. They represent a development "problem", and an awesome one at that.

While substantial progress has been made in India in reducing the percentage of the rural population below nationally defined poverty line, the absolute number of the rural poor has increased. The growth of output did not bring about a significant improvement in the income share of the lowest nor an uniform reduction in the percentage of the rural population below the poverty line. The situation actually worsened. Less than half of the rural population in India has access to safe water or sanitation, and only 60 per cent had any access to health services. National data on life expectancy, infant mortality and literacy show improvements, but also the persistence of completely unacceptable conditions.

The pursuit of growth has not solved the development problem. Trickle-down has not worked or it has not worked enough. The massive persistence of poverty, particularly in rural areas represents a problem for the popular acceptance of continued economic adjustment; and it represents a problem for growth itself. The problem lies not only in the unintended consequences of the prevailing development paradigm, but in the viability of the paradigm itself. Part of the debt crisis arose from an inability to mobilize fully domestic assets, and from systematic resort to external resources. The unsustainability of this form of development has been amply demonstrated. Part of the answer to the challenge of development lies in a greater and more appropriate use of the resources of developing countries themselves.

A substantial part of these assets can be created by the poor who have been so marginal to past development efforts. The poverty of a nation and the poverty of people are not as easily separable as was often thought in the past. In many cases, it is difficult to envisage national growth without strong economic development among the poor themselves—not us objects, but as subjects of development. The fact that this is insufficiently perceived is as much an expression of the development of social and economic interests as it is of the development or otherwise of economic theory. Development has frequently been associated with large-scale production and large-scale inputs of capital, and these new social and economic patterns have often defined development in their own image, i.e., in terms of he centrality of large-scale production and accumulation.

## Poverty Alleviation

The perspective is not that growth achieved by the better-off will pull the poor out of poverty, but that the mobilisation and enhancement of the resources and activities of the poor themselves can uphold their dignity and free them from the shackles of misery, while at the same time making a vital contribution to overall sustainable growth.

Individually and collectively, the obstacles facing the poor are formidable. They are, however, not insuperable. Most of the forces creating poverty are essentially social. They reflect systems of resources allocation that are made by societies, and as such they can be reversed. Pricing policies, credit systems, and social and productive services, which neglect the poor, as well as gender discrimination, are not natural, universal and inevitable facts—and neither is the poverty they give rise to. One of the major obstacles to overcome in fighting poverty is the perception of poverty itself—and of the poor. In this regard, perhaps the most important point is that the poor are not idle, they work. Nobody is simply "poor". In other words, it is not just a state of being. In this regard, "poor" is more aptly used as an adjective rather than as a noun. The rural poor are poor farmers, poor herders and poor fishermen. In short, they are poor producers: their incomes are gained from their work. The answer to poverty lies in creating the conditions for them to earn more from their work. From this perspective, overcoming poverty does not mean less growth, it is a contributor to growth—for it means making the poor more productive. Too often in the past poverty alleviation has been seen as a burden on the economy, as involving a transfer of something for nothing in exchange. It need not be that way: it can be an investment in production, benefiting both poor and the national economy. Poverty has been defined as a production problem, and poverty alleviation as an investment.

Nobody wishes to be poor, and few accept it passively. The poor are rarely without initiative. What they lack are the means of pursuing it. In no small measure, overcoming poverty involves building upon this initiative and will, helping organize cooperation, and providing material support. This support does not have to take the form of handouts. The problem of the poor is not that they cannot handle resources efficiently, but they do not have access to them.

The challenge of creating an institutional framework for credit for the poor is an expression of the general institutional challenge facing poverty alleviation: institutions are not oriented to the poor. Many factors enter into this, ranging from the costs of working with a large number of unorganized people, to the prevalence of myths about the improvidence of the poor, to a simple desire on the part of the better-off to monopolize scarce resources. The answer to this is to create institutional responsiveness, either through introducing demand-led organisation into existing institutions concerned with the poor or through promoting institutions created by the poor themselves. In both cases, participation by the poor is critical. The objective is not only to mobilize the individual initiatives of the poor, but also to mobilize their collective strength and capabilities. As individuals, many of the poor are virtually unreachable. As members of associations and groups they create their own channels for institutional access.

The poor as producers; the poor as credit-worthy handlers of material assistance; the poor as institutional actors—these are not elements of theory, but of practice and experience. Notwithstanding the growing acceptance of the need to do something "about" the poor, not everyone shares this understanding of poverty. As long as the poor are viewed from afar, the myths of poverty and the poor persist. Even those who over emphasize the need for social "safety nets" and handouts, while ostensibly helping the poor, maintain the image of helplessness, and of the need to do something "for" them. A closer view reveal something very different: tremendous work and initiative on the part of the poor, both based on their desire to do something for themselves. This is not a burden, it is an extraordinary social and economic asset. Again, viewed from a distance, poverty looks overwhelming. The closer view reveals very specific situations of opportunities and needs. These can be responded to—not only through soup kitchens, which should be seen as desirable in addressing emergencies only—but through strengthening the individual and collective means available to the poor to carve out their own path of independence and growth. The dynamics of poverty are reversible, but only in collaboration with the poor themselves.

Precisely because of past neglect of the poor as producers, a neglect involving a failure to involve them in the process of technological development, organisation, and capitalisation, the gap between the current and potential production of the poor is enormous. Investment in the poor is not a loss-making enterprise. Poverty is less a failure of the poor, than a failure of policy-makers to grasp their potential. Far from there being a tradeoff between poverty and growth, the persistence of poverty represents a limit to growth.

Mobilizing and enhancing the ability of the rural poor to expand their own income and contribute to national growth is not simply a process of raising incomes. It involves structural change in economies and societies. It involves helping the poor to position themselves securely within main-line economic processes. This means first increasing and improving their access to land—by land reform, land-titling, better management and better conservation, supported, where necessary, by irrigation, new technologies and improved infrastructure. Secondly, it means increasing the productivity and use of rural labour, emphasizing labour intensive technology and better training for new skills. Thirdly, it means making more capital available to the rural poor, mobilizing savings, providing infrastructure and developing financial services tailored to their situation and needs.

Not least, it mean acknowledging the important contribution of poor women in all of these areas of activity. At present, the contribution of women to the rural economy is seriously underestimated—the "invisible women" syndrome. Official statistics rarely make any effort to measure it, even though it is more than clear that not just unpaid household work but the farm and trading activities of women make a vital and significant contribution to the well-being of poor rural households. All the evidence suggests that the poorer the household the more hour's women work and the greater their investment in both economic production and family welfare. From a situation of multiple disadvantage as poor, as women and often as single parents, women can move to one in which they contribute and benefit three-fold—in the home, in society at large and, not least, in the development of the next generation.

Many of the measure that need to be taken to allow the poor to realize their potential do not involve more expenditures; they involve the elimination of economic distortions against the rural poor. These distortions have effectively taxed the poor, and mainly the rural poor, in favour of inappropriate and inefficient urban developments whose support has been at the root of widespread economic crises. To no small extent, helping the poor make their potential contribution to development involves no more than creating a "level playing field" and, when conceived in such a light, structural adjustment can make a vital contribution to both resumed growth and social equity. It is often felt that the poor are somehow "outside" the scope of national economic policies. This is virtually never the case. They are affected by national economic policies, but this inclusion takes a very special form: exposure to the costs, and exclusion from the benefits. In this regard, there is a certain irony in the view that small-scale producers "need" subsidies to survive. In fact, it has been the development of large-scale production in agriculture (and industry) in India that has been heavily dependent upon subsidisation over the decades—benefits, which small-scale producers have rarely enjoyed.

This is characteristic of many forms of large-scale production in India—although nominally at the cutting edge of efficiency and productivity; it is they rather than the small-scale producers who have been dependent upon transfers and protection for their reproduction.

Change in the environment of poverty necessitates greater awareness of the root causes of poverty on the part of policy-makers. However, the realisation of the social and economic potential of the rural poor is not just a question of economic policy and investment. It also involves the development of a general social framework in which the economic and social interests of the poor can be freely articulated and responded to. It means instilling democratic and participatory values at every level in society and not just at the level of nationwide institutions. The most valid spokesmen of the poor are the poor themselves.

The opening of economic and social opportunities to the poor offers the possibility of more stable and sustainable change. The alternative is for societies to polarize further, for the welfare burden to grow to greater proportions and for a widening gap to develop between the modern and traditional sectors. In the end, the continued poverty of the rural areas will be a brake on the output of the advanced sector, eroding the potential for self-sustaining growth.

# 9 Employment and Poverty Alleviation

Today the key socio-economic problem is large-scale unemployment. Spreading joblessness brings many other problems in its wake. It erodes national incomes and living standards, aggravating the already grindingly difficult job of promoting development and alleviating poverty. Joblessness also raises government budget deficits, increasing macro-economic instability while soaking up investment for productive capital expenditure, education, training and relief aid. And joblessness ruins lives and communities by depriving people of the dignity and satisfaction that comes with earning one's keep and making a contribution to the well-being of family and society.

Theories about how best to nurture development (and thus create jobs) have shifted considerably over the last decade. The state rôle has evolved, in the minds of many, from being a source of relief for the problems of unemployment, poverty and underdevelopment, to being a fundamental cause of these problems through the distorting impact of its intervention on the market.

However, the more market-oriented philosophy that grew up during the 1990s has yet to provide convincing solutions in practice at least not on a grand scale and especially not in terms of job creation as the present jobless economic recovery demonstrates.

The weakness of the current recovery and past approaches to economic development can be traced to the failure to consider employment as the predominant means of promoting growth and alleviating poverty. In policy circles it has too long been an almost ignored priority.

Current trends thus bode poorly, particularly as unemployment rates soar. In light of the circumstances, we need to begin re-examining some of the fundamental questions—if only to find out what has gone wrong with the answers.

## Minimum Wage?

Let's begin with wages. With corporate restructuring in full force on a global scale, are low wage rates required to raise employment and maximize profits? A top manager of a multinational consumer electronics group certainly thinks so; he likened the perfect factory to a ship "so that we could move it around the world to where labour was cheapest". Perhaps, but this bottom-line emphasis on unit labour costs ignores at least two other factors; namely, that higher wages can act as a screen to select more productive workers and that higher wages translate into better productivity via improved worker nutrition, increased consumption and a generally healthier quality of life.

If higher wages being these benefits (and it is an open question) should government insist that there be a minimum wage rate? Neo-classical economists tend to respond "no", assuming that a higher wage rate puts money into the pockets of some low wage workers while forcing many others out of work because companies cannot afford to pay them.

## Technology Transfer

The impact of technology is another area in need of study. Technological innovation is usually labour-saving and tends to originate in industrialized countries, moving toward developing countries like India, Pakistan where labour tends to be low cost and abundant. Would it therefore make sense to slow down or somehow restrict technology transfer, especially to development markets, in the interest of preserving employment?

The answer here is clearly—No. Historical evidence abundantly demonstrates that attempts to retard technological progress bring about greater poverty and lower growth. Technology, infact, is at the heart of the new endogenous growth theory which is very much in vogue among development economists today. Slowing down or inhibiting technology transfer would certainly dash many countries' development hopes and aggravate poverty. However, the relationship between technology, development, employment and poverty alleviation is not without its complications.

In the 1980s, the buzz word among development specialists was "appropriate technology", i.e., small-scale and labour-intensive technologies that would increase productive output while allowing an equilibrium solution to be found such that the ratio of the productivity of labour to that of capital is proportional to their relative prices. The conditions for this "small is beautiful" approach to technology tended to be best met in agricultural production. However, where manufacturing industry is concerned, the small-is-beautiful approach foundered badly when the only viable technological alternatives proved to be highly capital-intensive.

## Development Gap

A wide gap has emerged between developing countries with an inward focus (which tended to be protectionist and pursue policies of import substitution) and those with an outward focus and a policy of pursuing export-led growth. Competing in international markets requires technology that is as good as or better than that found in advanced, industrialized nations. Small, therefore, is not beautiful in the global manufacturing economy where product standards are high and the elasticity of substitution between labour and capital is very limited.

The drive to obtain state-of-the-art technology thus leads to a policy conundrum: it is a pre-condition for success in manufactured exports, but the impulse to compete successfully in this most lucrative sector speeds up the transfer of technology from the developed to the developing world, thus reinforcing the bias toward labour saving equipment in developing countries and accelerating a process that is seen as a source of job loss in the industrialized countries.

## Technology and Jobs

Before concluding that modern technology transfer is inimical to employment in developing countries, we have to distinguish clearly between technology's static and dynamic consequences. In a static sense, it is true that highly capital-intensive export industries may not create much employment on a net basis, but the dynamic effects of technology transfer do contribute to economic growth. And growth, in turn, generates multiplier effects in the form of demand, which stimulates ancillary production activities (like food processing or consumer goods) that rely on more labour-intensive technologies.

The problem is that the diffusion and application of technology on a global scale blurs the categories of international product specialisation and creates a much more competitive and conflict-prone international environment.

For example, we have already seen the Asian Tigers move from producing goods such as textiles and processed food to producing hi-tech and value-added consumer durables. This advance is only possible due to the growth of human capital (facilitated by investment and higher incomes) and it leaves production of textiles to other industrializing countries, like Indonesia, the Philippines and now China. But the dynamic comes at the expense of jobs in industrialized regions, like the US and the EC, which lost more than a quarter of their work force in textiles during the 1980s. In spite of job losses, advanced countries continue to produce textiles, notwithstanding major differences in the hourly wage rates for spinning and weaving and the fact that essentially the same hi-tech equipment is being used in most production centres.

## Protectionism

What has happened in textiles is happening in other industrial sectors (automobiles, for example) as well. The intense market competition is providing to be a source of trade conflicts, and possibly protectionism, as jobs come under increasing pressure.

For many workers and managers, the benefits of foreign direct investment look increasingly like a zero-sum game for employment, and there is a real risk that the tenuous link between overall growth and employment will break down altogether. It is hardly surprising that we are already seeing negatively affected workers and local businesses clamouring for protection in advanced countries.

## Governments, Role

The concerned governments are suppose to carry out much of this research. The three initial lines of inquiry follow from three reasonable assumptions about the future.

- First, increase in welfare and consumption subsidies are out; investments in training and human capital are in. How can investments in human capital be directed to positive employment effects? Is it perhaps not time to explore more fully benefit schemes targeting the unemployed and the unskilled poor providing them with the type of subsidies that would enhance their human capital, improve their health and productivity through better nutrition and preventive medicine, and restore the dignity of holding a job?
- Second, given the quasi-inevitability of increased automation in manufacturing, how can other sectors (particularly agriculture and services) be developed to export their long-term potential for employment creation?
- Third, given the inevitable pressures of work and productivity in the global economy, what sort of alternative institutional arrangements need to evolve with respect to industrial relations, employment and work conditions?

Finding answers to these and other questions will require no small amount of new thinking, but parochialism or a failure of imagination would be fatal flaws in this global era.

# 10 Peace and Poverty

Peace should not be understood in military terms, like absence of armed conflicts. Peace should be understood in a human way in abroad social, political and economic way. Peace should mean social justice between nations and within nations. It should mean establishment of human rights for all people.

In the new context the concept of "peace" would be the existence of a political and economic environment where each individual human beings is truly free; free from the control of any powerful person or any powerful nation, free from poverty, hunger and indignities, each individual human being free to explore the limits of one's potential.

Today peace is threatened, more than anything else, by poverty, unjust social and economic order, absence of democracy and environmental degradation.

The cold war cloud has gone. You can feel the breath of fresh air around the world. Now there is no visible competitor left for capitalism. It is quite risky to live with a philosophy, which has no challenger. To be safe, we must go to the essence of the philosophy of capitalism rather than be satisfied with the practices, which emerged over years through patchworks of expediency.

Contrary to common belief, it is not the "free enterprise" which is the essence of capitalism. It is the freedom of individual thought and freedom of individual action which is the essence of capitalism. It is these freedoms which support free enterprise, free trade, free circulation of capital, and free circulation of people.

We must work out a new system, appropriate for the new world, from the basics of capitalism, not from the practices of capitalism. Many of these practices take away freedom, rather than guarantee it. Traps must go. People cannot remain trapped in places where they cannot live because of ecological, political, or economic reasons. This planet belongs to all people. If some people are trapped somewhere, we must all come forward to remove the causes of their discomfort. At the same time we must leave our shores open for anybody who decides to join us, or any body who decides to part our company.

Poverty denies a person control over his destiny. Poverty means not being able to tell what tomorrow would be like. If we examine the situation carefully we'll see that the poverty is neither created by the poor, nor sustained by the poor. It is the system of policies and institutions that we have built around us that creates and sustains poverty. Poverty is the denial of human rights. Over one billion people live below the absolute poverty line right now on this planet, are denied of almost all human rights. There is no way one can defend the existence of poverty anywhere. Poverty is a disgrace for the entire mankind. Because we allow another human being to die of hunger, or malnutrition, or common curable diseases, or exposure to climate, we are reduced to less human beings. If a particular world system is responsible for creating this massive poverty we must act to replace it.

Resource-wise or technology-wise, there is no reason why poverty should exist and continue to deepen and widen. If we make up our minds to wipe out poverty from the surface of the earth, the worst aspect of poverty can be removed within the next couple of decades.

We can build a poverty-free world at a fraction of the cost of what we spend on war preparations. Nations become very generous when it comes to making their war-machine heftier in the name of ensuring "peace". Can we persuade ourselves to allocate a part of our time, money and intellect to achieve peace by making the people at the bottom the winners, rather than nations winning wars? "Peace" achieved by winning wars is earned by destroying people. The real peace can be achieved by building people, by reinforcing people, by helping people to reach their potential. Removing poverty is the process of building people.

Each human being is a wonderful creation of the Creator. Each human being is born with great potentials. Poverty denies any opportunity for a person to achieve any of his/her potential. We have built a world system, which is in the habit of pushing people down not building them up. It creates barriers around individuals, rather than remove them.

The most effective step that we must take to remove poverty is to create a system, which creates enabling conditions for people and removes the existing barriers. The institutional barriers were skillfully crafted over the centuries to benefit a handful of people.

Resource-poor nations with high incidence of poverty waste away enormous human capability each day by denying poor people the use of their energy and ingenuity. If they could have been made economically active, not only they could have contributed in the national production, they would have helped expand the domestic market for the products produced. The poor can be transformed into the engine of growth if we only allow them to unleash their capacity.

We cannot be at peace with ourselves if we know there is a human being who lives a life worse than an animal. A human being is supposed to live differently than an animal. He/she is supposed to live a life with human dignity. Human dignity is what distinguishes a human being from an animal. When we cannot ensure this dignity for others, our own dignity becomes an empty pretense.

There must be a thousand and one ways to remove poverty from the earth. We may or may not know some of those ways already. Obviously there are many more ways yet to be designed, each more effectively than others. When we shall find them, how many of them we shall find, how quickly we find them; will depend on how eager we are to find them. But to say that poverty cannot be overcome, directly and quickly, is to underestimate the capacity of human mind.

Poverty is homogeneous only when considered from the point of view of income or consumption: the uniformity of the poor as a category exists only on the level of the fact that they have little to consume. When considered from the point of view of production, i.e., the circumstances in which the poor must operate to gain their income, the conditions of poverty are extraordinary diverse. A concrete grasp of these diverse circumstances is the first step in developing relevant instruments to address not only the problems of the poor, but also the challenge of taking advantage of the opportunities available to them.

The conventional means of measuring economic progress, such as Gross National Product per capita, tell us little about the real nature of poverty. In recent years this sort of yardstick has been supplemented by measurements of food security, income distribution, and social development (encompassing health and education). These offer the possibility of composite indices, allowing the development of more rounded characterisations and comparisons of poverty at the national level. However, these principally refer to the symptoms of poverty, not to the relational factors generating it. Poverty is not a state of being; it is the effect of dynamic processes. While it is important to know where poverty is greatest, it is critical to know why it exists. This inquiry necessarily leads away from the nature of the poor as individuals to the nature of their social and physical environment. Poverty is not only a personal phenomenon, it is a social status. As such, while its effects can be measured on the level of the individual, its causes must be sought elsewhere. From the point of view of poverty alleviation the process of becoming is just as important as the state of being.

At the heart of poverty is the inadequate access of the poor to productive resources. Low income tends to reflect inadequate means of production, not incompetent producers. However, poverty in India is not simply a reflection of private resources. A broad range of "external" factors impinge on incomes, among them the following:

## National Policies

One of the ironies of Indian development is that while no government wants poverty, many policies contribute to it—what is given in anti-programmes is drained away by other policies. The poor do not always come out ahead in the balance—they are often net "donor" to the rest of society. Frequent reference is made to unsustainable forms of development—to urban over-expansion, industrialisation based on subsidies, and to public sector engorgement. What is less frequently realized is that the bill for these phenomena is often presented to the rural poor. Taxation of exports to sustain sectors with little export potential of their own and subsidized food imports to supply the urban population are policies that are often paid for by the rural poor. In many areas of India, exports are agricultural goods produced by small farmers. Here export taxes contribute to rural poverty. The same is true of "cheap" food imports, which depress the prices paid to small farmers for their food crops.

"Structural imbalance" is not only a recipe for increasing external indebtedness; it is also a recipe for increasing the poverty of the rural population. The political weakness of the poor in most areas is not only the basis for inadequate poverty alleviation programmes and policies—it is the basis for an actual transfer of their income to more socially influential groups. While it is often correctly asserted that the poor are the first to suffer from adjustments involving public social expenditure cuts, it is often the case that they also have the most to gain from the elimination of policy-based economic distortions that reflect social power rather than productive efficiency and potential.

## Demographic Factors

Accelerated population growth is a long-term contributor to poverty. In India the incomes of the poor have declined, mortality rates are also falling, pushing the numbers up. In the meantime, land is becoming scarcer, plots more fragmented and the soil and pasture increasingly degraded. This phenomenon is not without its policy dimensions. As long as the poor remain undercapitalized, and essential determinant of household income is the amount of labour available to it household economic strategies favour large families. While population policy has a role to play, possibly more critical is a change in the economic environment. Access to capital and more secure income changes perceptions of the need for labour. In the medium- and long-term, population dynamics are driven by the underlying productive systems. As long as the production systems of the poor remain underdeveloped, population growth remains high, restricting even the future possibility of development.

## Natural Resource Management and the Environment

If poverty is both cause and effect of rapid population expansion, so poverty is both cause and effect of many dimensions of degradation of the environment. Many of the rural poor, but by no means all, live in areas of extreme environmental fragility, a circumstance often prompted by high level of control by the better-off over more stable and productive resource areas. Here the poor are extraordinarily exposed to the dangers of erosion, whittling away at an already meager productive base. The threat is not entirely due to nature. Rather, poverty accelerates erosion. Without capital, the poor are frequently unable to invest in even traditional methods of soil and water conservation. And without sufficient land they are forced to shorten fallow periods, putting further strain on the resource base. As in the case of population growth, the result is strain not only on the poor, but on the entire Indian economy. Given the extremely limited economic alternatives, the solution to this problem is not to forbid the use of environmentally fragile resources to the poor; it is to change the conditions under which their use takes place. Access to conservation technology is important; but more so are security of land tenure and resources to invest.

Combating poverty means not only increasing the production of the poor, but also preserving and enhancing the long-term value of the resource they control. What this very often means, in practice is assisting the poor in reestablishing a stable relationship with fragile resource. Prevailing processes in many areas involve the gradual—and sometimes not so gradual—depletion of natural resources, to the detriment of all. Part of he answer to this is conservation. Part of the answer is also to provide viable economic alternatives to the poor, reducing their dependence on erosion-prone crop and livestock practices.

## Exploitative Intermediates

The poor are not unaware of the pressure upon them, and also of means of overcoming them. Their ability to respond, however, is severely impaired by social powerlessness. The poor are surrounded by a dense network of public and private factors reducing their freedom of action, and actually draining what few resources they do have. Members of the network include traders and moneylenders capitalizing upon the economic weakness of the poor, and engaging them in unequal exchanges. They also include public agencies either indifferent to the requirements of the socially uninfluential, or actively engaged in extracting "surplus" for use by other groups. Not to be excluded from this are organisations which are ostensibly "for" the poor, but which, in fact, serve as systems of containment and control.

# 11 For Richer, For Fairer: *Poverty Reduction and Income Distribution*

Will the international target of reducing poverty by half over the next 15 years be met? Not unless growth efforts are accompanied by significant improvements in income distribution. Poverty reduction is a twin function of the rate of growth and of changes in income distribution. The research shows better distribution has as much impact on reducing poverty as had increased growth. And given predicted rates of economic growth, it emerges as the factor that will make the main difference between success and failure for new 'pro-poor' growth strategies.

Over the past decade, the amount of poverty reduction resulting from a given rate on economic growth has varied in close step with income distribution. On average, a growth rate of 10 per cent reduced the poverty headcount (the percentage of people living on less than $ 1 a day) by 9 per cent in countries where income was fairly equally distributed. However in countries where income was unequally distributed, a growth rate of 10 per cent reduced the poverty headcount by only 3 per cent.

The World Bank estimated that developing countries will grow at 4 per cent per capita per annum until 2015. So the good news is that the income-poverty target is attainable provided that significant improvements take place in income, distribution. These can be achieved ex-ante, by designing growth strategies that increase disproportionately the incomes of the poorest or ex-post, by redistributing income through taxation. Many questions arise. What is the recipe for income-redistributing growth? Is there a trade-off between growth and distribution? An ex-post strategies of reduction feasible? These questions are far from new. Indeed, to a large degree, they are the very questions on which the development studies profession is founded. Nevertheless, they have been neglected in recent years. Does current research offer new perspectives? Articles in this issue of insights offer six main conclusions. They are that:

- We need a way to measure 'pro-poor growth.' The concept originates from the 1990 World Development Report of the World Bank and is taken to mean a labour intensive growth path that encompasses the economic activities of the poor. However, such a growth path could be accompanied by increasing, declining or static income inequality. Mc Culloch and Baulch propose that the 'poverty bias of growth or PBG (whether pro poor or not) be defined by comparing actual change in income distribution with the change that would have resulted had all incomes grown at one rate with no change to income inequality. This difference is compared in their report (opposite) for two states in India. From this comparison it emerges that growth in Bihar State was accompanied by worsening income distribution and has been biased against the poor, whereas in Andhra Pradesh the reverese was true.

- Growth might be expected to be pro-poor if it takes place in areas and sectors where the poor live and work. For the poorest countries this means mostly in rural areas and to all large extent in agriculture. In Asia, Green Revolution technologies were adopted by poor farmers because they were scale-neutral and low-risk. Poor non-farmers also benefited from the extra employment and lower food prices that resulted. In Sub-Saharan Africa, the Green Revolution has been slower in coming, but research at Reading by Mosley suggests an African Green Revolution will help. In Uganda, for example, the spread of new technologies in maize and cassava has contributed to sharp falls in poverty, notable in the country's North where mosaic resistant cassava has made a conspicuous difference to farmer's yields and incomes in an otherwise poor and undeveloped region.

- Even so, as many will remember well from debates about the Green Revolution in Asia, not everybody benefits from growth. In Ethiopia, researchers from the Universities of Oxford and Addis Ababa found that rural poverty has fallen sharply since the change of government in 1992, driven by market liberalisation and better weather (see Dercon, backfold). Yet those who have gained have been those with assets, including land, oxen for ploughing, edcuation and access to public goods such as roads. Those without assets are left behind. Rural inequality has actually risen, implying Ethiopia could reduce poverty faster if policies countered inequality yet maintained current growth rates.
- People without assets might be expected to compensate by migrating or moving out of agriculture. Sometimes this happens, but seeking off-farm opportunities may be easier of the haves tan the have-nots. In rural Zimbabwe, for example, Piesse and Thirtle have shown that (in more remote areas at least) those with higher farm incomes are better placed to exploit off-farm opportunities, including the option of working in town.
- In any case, migration to town may not offer much to the unskilled—again, a problem facing those without assets. The evidence here comes from China, in research carried out by the institute of Economics and Statistics. Wage employment has increased in urban China, but wage inequality has increased sharply, with falling real wages for the unskilled.
- The efficiency (hence the growth) and equity trade-off is far from clear cut. Analysis by Knight of the reasons behind rising wage-income inequality in China has revealed that some of these changes reflect greater labour market efficiency. In other words, more productive, experienced and skilled worker have become better paid. Other changes hint a new inefficiencies creeping into China's labour market, such as growing labour market, such as growing

> discrimination: females and minority groups find they are disadvantaged in the labour market, whereas members of the Communist Party are more likely to get jobs. Other signs are sharper segmentation, with state employees paid more than private sector counterparts and growing differences in wage rates between the provinces, not offset by labour mobility.

The cross-section of findings offered in these pages does not amount to a systematic review of the inequality question' in developing countries. Far from it: here is fertile ground for further research. Even so, we are confident that it is time to promote inequality to the fore of the research and policy agenda.

# 12 Can Economic Growth Reduce Poverty?

## New Findings on Inequality, Economic Growth and Poverty

Many people still think first of 'economic growth' in relation to poverty reduction. Indeed, their correlation is one of the mot-discussed issues of combating poverty. The relationship is of great importance because if there is a clear causal dependency, reducing poverty could fundamentally be limited to measures to promote growth. However, if there was low growth or stagnation it would not be possible to reduce poverty decisively. In the opposite case, that of the phenomena having no causal relation, promising measures to reduce poverty could be taken up even without economic growth.

Hardly anyone now explicitly expresses the view that economic development trickles down automatically to the poor. Practical experience has refuted this assumption dating from the early days of development policy in the 1960s. However, a number of studies show development of growth and a decline in poverty running parallel. On the other hand, there are also examples which show that despite high economic growth, poverty is not reduced markedly. The common answer to the question this raises is thus: Yes, growth can reduce poverty, but only if additional measures oriented on the poor are taken up. This is often termed pro-poor growth. But what that means in detail, and whether economic growth as such plays a causal role at all, is not clarified. It is worth taking a look at the arguments on the basis of more recent empirical and theoretical knowledge.

## No Direct Causality between Growth and Poverty Reduction

Among the many indicators of poverty, the income of the poor (income poverty) has the closest relationship to economic growth. An increase in gross domestic product and thus national income could, if other factors come into play be linked with an increase in the per capita income of the poor.

Such a relationship between economic growth and the income of the poor, however, cannot be described as causal, as is asserted implicitly time and again by the statement that growth is a necessary but not sufficient precondition for poverty reduction. In so far as growth and poverty reduction arise at the same time at the end of a process, they exist alongside each other. It would be almost a tautology to say that the former is the cause or part-cause of the latter. Both express the same thing, namely a change in per capita income as well, and both have similar causes. What matters is recognising what these causes are and what specific factors must come into play so that the income of the poor grows too. Growth as a "prerequisite" or "condition" is then no longer the focus; the priority is asking for specific policies that result in higher incomes for the poor. The detour in thinking about growth is not necessary. Since, however, it is based on similar factors, such as fiscal policy/budget structure, employment policy, combating inflation, and institutional development, economic growth can also emerge if poverty is reduced. The difference of views lies in the fact that under the heading 'poverty reduction' the aim is no longer growth, but a purposeful reduction of poverty.

Therefore, in reverse, successful combating of poverty can be seen as being the cause of growth insofar as activating the capabilities of the poor and using their productive capacity of the poor and using their productive capacity triggers economic drive.

## Indirect Causality between Growth and Poverty Reduction?

So even if economic growth fundamentally has no direct causal impact on poverty, growth still can reduce it indirectly. This is the case when due to positive economic development a government has greater revenue and uses the surplus for combating poverty, for example by providing such public goods as education and health services. Also in these cases, however, growth is not a compelling precondition. Even without growth greater government revenue can be achieved, for example by more efficient tax collection. And leeway for social welfare spending can be gained by redistributing the budget, such as by cutting military appropriations. Furthermore, an automatic process is not given because the government can also use surplus funds for non-social purposes.

Creation of jobs due to increased economic activity can be another indirect link between economic growth and income poverty, if such a development generates income and reduces poverty. But also in this case I see no compelling causality because, for instance, industrial jobs are not necessarily open to the really poor. In addition, these positive impacts occur to a considerable extent only in the event of labour-intensive development. In many countries, however, economic growth is achieved by capital-intensive production.

## Inequality, Growth and Income Poverty

If national incomes, grow, a naïve observer might assume that the income of the poor must also grow along with it. But that would be a statistical fallacy. Even if only the income of the rich grows, this results in macro-economics statistics showing a higher per capita income. What the true conditions are is shown as soon as one divides the population statistically into income groups, such as in fifths, as is usual. It then turns out that the bald figures on average per capita growth can certainly cloak a situation where the income of the richest fifth of the population is growing fast while that of the poorest fifth is stagnating. Despite growth, the gap between the two becomes even wider.

The unequal distribution of income (and of other assets such as property and access to social services), and its connection to poverty reduction and growth has recently returned to the forefront of the debate.

It is obvious that inequality and its changes have direct effects on the poverty situation. Does inequality also have an impact on poverty via its relation to growth, because growth promotes or reduces inequality? Earlier, the predominant view was that rapid growth was linked with at least a temporary increase in inequality, so that a distinct policy of growth initially disadvantaged the poor.

The current dominant view is that growth has no foreseeable effects on inequality and that inequality changes only very slowly, in reverse, however, it is assumed that greater equality is a determinant of growth. According to that view, an indirect relationship between poverty on one side and inequality as a factor dependent upon growth on the other is not given.

That leads to the conclusion that fair distribution has more weight than growth. Fair distribution, however, does not depend upon growth. An appropriate policy is possible at any time, not only after an economic situation has improved. The notion that still shimmers through the debate that "something must be earned first before it can be distributed", is wrong. It is a matter of designing policy and the entire economic process right from the start in such a way that the surplus benefits all including the poor. Important elements of such a policy are, for example, land reform and development of finance systems.

## Relationship of Growth to Poverty

According to today's conventional wisdom, income poverty expresses only a part of what poverty means. Not least through the voices of the poor themselves, it has become clear that violation of human dignity and rights, a lack of participation in decisions and exclusion from society, unequal treatment of men and women, and vulnerability are also regarded as poverty. For poverty is caused to a great degree by conflicts of power and interests. Income poverty often is not even seen as the greatest problem.

What relationship do these more far reaching characteristics of poverty have to economic growth? A direct relationship of growth to socially-related aspects such as women's inheritance rights, land rights and exclusion from decisions cannot be seen. Considerable improvements in favour of the poor can be achieved here even without economic growth.

Those who see a strong and causal connection between economic growth and poverty reduction must ask themselves what the prospects are for high growth rates and thus for a decline in poverty. Coupling poverty reduction to economic growth is problematic. If only low growth rates are to be expected.

Another question is whether continuous increases in growth are at all desirable and possible in the medium to long term. In this connection, a difference should perhaps be made between developing countries and industrialised nations. But environmental compatibility and availability of resources set limits to growth for both. Some academics assume that industrialised nations have already reached an inherent limit (stagnation theory) and that the high growth rates of earlier years will not return. Moreover, they add, full employment is no longer achievable due to, among other things, an ongoing increase in productivity, and current unemployment cannot be reduced by customary means. In any case, if growth were to be taken as the major benchmark, the prospects for a radical reduction of income poverty around the world would be modest.

## Summing Up

Poverty is a complex problem and reducing it depends upon many interconnected factors that is why poverty cannot be attributed to one main cause nor its reduction based on one main strategy. Economic growth is just one strategic element among many others related to poverty reduction. An indirect causal connection between growth and poverty reduction can only be seen because governments will have a grater scope for action due to economic growth, and if they promote labour-intensive development.

Therefore growth's role in poverty reduction must be put into perspective growth cannot be the first thing that comes to mind, nor is it the golden path to reducing poverty. The simplistic theory of economic growth as the main condition obstructs the bigger picture; it clings to the underlying and ongoing belief in the trickle-down effect. Even if there is no growth or for inherent reasons there can be none, there are promising ways to take on the challenge of mass poverty in the developing countries. Up front, governments and bilateral and multilateral donors must have the political will to design economic, financial and social policies so that they are oriented on poverty in a coherent way—the result can also be economic growth.

# 13 Democracy and Poverty: *Are they Interlinked?*

Democracy assistance and poverty reduction are rightly becoming two focal and related—issues for development assistance. Increasingly, many organisations, including intergovernmental, national and civil society, are focusing their work on these two areas. Futhermore, the relationship between these two issues is complex and ever changing. There is thus a need to develop methodologies of linking democracy assistance and poverty reduction at both the policy and programme levels. International IDEA (Institute for Democracy and Electoral Assistance) in cooperation with the World Bank and the United Nations Development Programme, is developing concrete strategies that address these two objectives in a mutually reinforcing way. Through an overall situation analysis followed by regional meetings in sub-Saharan Africa, South Asia, Latin America, the Caucasus and the Arab region, the Institute has marshalled evidence of some of the key problems that affect democracy consolidation and poverty reduction in these countries:

- Corruption and its undermining effect on popular confidence in public institutions;
- Continuing economic instability coupled with the lack of strategies for addressing the twin challenges of poverty and increasing popular participation in its alleviation;
- The extremely limited nature of citizen's influence on overall policy and decision-making processes despite the spread of formal democratic institutions;

- A trend in many post-communist states towards viewing growing poverty as a direct consequence of a transition to democracy.

In short, the evidence is not very encouraging for the prospects for democracy consolidation and poverty reduction. The critical step, International IDEA, advocates is the development of an approach that not only seeks to put democracy assistance and poverty reduction on top of the development assistance agenda, but also to encourage all involved to treat them as twin elements of an integrated programme of action.

Through a focus on accountable governance, promotion and protection of citizenship and rights and increased popular participation, International IDEA believes that both democracy and poverty reduction can be addressed simultaneously. Policy recommendations are being developed and will be shared in the course of this year with governments, international organisations and civil society bodies.

International IDEA believes that democracy promotion can be used as a tool for fulfilling a variety of objectives. Democracy matters because it protects human right and preserves human dignity. But democracy also matters because it helps to address some of the most critical challenges facing states today: peace, development, economic growth and stability.

Democracy does not guarantee any one of these, but increasingly it seems to be a precondition for them in the long term. Thus, advocating democracy goes beyond being a moral issue; it becomes *fundamental* to advancing the well-being of people and the stability of states. International IDEA will continue to explore the link between democracy and the major issues facing society today and continue to argue the case democracy.

# 14 Taking Poverty to Heart:
## *Non-Communicable Diseases and the Poor*

Non-Communicable Diseases (NCDs) are the leading cause of death worldwide. Their emergence as the predominant health problem in wealthy countries accompanied economic development. As a result, NCDs are often referred to as 'diseases of affluence'. But is this a misleading term? It suggests that these are not major problems for the world's poor, which is quite simply wrong, as this article illustrates. Is it time to rethink policy on NCDs?

NCDs include cardiovascular disease (CVD), such as stroke and heart attack, diabetes, chronic lung disease, cancer, diseases of bones and joints, and mental illness. The single biggest killer is coronary heart disease, followed by other CVDs, cancer and chronic lung disease. Diabetes is a major contributor to deaths from CVD, but also causes its own unique complications. Common risk factors for these conditions include smoking, physical activity, obesity and diets high in saturated fat and sodium and low in fruit and vegetables.

By 2020, NDCs will be the biggest cause of death in all regions apart from sub-Saharan Africa. It is predicted that in 2010, the number of people with diabetes worldwide will be double the level in 1995 and that the biggest increase (both proportionately and in absolute number) will be in poorer regions. CVD occurs at an earlier age in developing countries, increasing the potential adverse economic and social consequences.

NCDs are already major health problems for adults in the poorest countries of the world. Demographic data show that age-specific death rates from NCDs in Tanzania are higher than in wealthier countries.Mortality rates for some NCDs, such as stroke, are particularly high. However, while NCDs account for 80 per cent of adult deaths in developed regions, the figure is less than 30 per cent in Tanzania, reflecting the continuing burden of infectious disease. Countries like Tanzania suffer the worst of both worlds'. Even within a country, 'diseases of affluence' is a misleading term. A more accurate label is 'diseases of Urbanisation'. Several studies from developing countries show increased levels of high blood pressure and other NCD risk factors in urban compared to rural populations. Even within urban areas, the more affluent do not always suffer the greatest burden.

The rise of NCDs in developing countries is inextricably linked to economic and cultural globalisation. This is exemplified by the activities of multinational tobacco companies. Tobacco-related deaths will exceed the toll due to HIV and become the single largest preventable cause of death by 2020. Curbing the effects of globalisation on the prevention and treatment of NCDs will also require regulation of food and agriculture multinationals and the pharmaceutical and healthcare industries.

Much of the projected rise in NCDs is preventable, particularly that due to smoking, poor diet, physical inactivity and obesity. Early action in some population could prevent the emergence of these risk factors altogether; in other, the challenge is to reduce established levels. Although it is unclear whether all major risk factors are equally important in every region, the strength and consistency of data on the core risk factors in several ethnic groups justify preventative action now.

Lessons from risk factor intervention studies in rich and middle income countries suggest that success requires:

- Broad intersectoral action;
- Community participation;
- Appropriate legislation;
- Involvement of appropriate NGOs;
- Health services changes—to manage those at high risk and promote public education.

Even apparently minor changes, such as a small fall in average population blood pressure, can have substantial benefits. However, some preventative pogrammes have produced disappointing results and almost all have failed to halt the ubiquitous increase in obesity. This highlights the difficulty of promoting healthy behaviour by individuals who are surrounded by barriers to change and inducements to lead an unhealthy lifestyle.

Health systems in developing countries face both a growing need for prevention programmes and increasing numbers of individuals requiring treatment. The complications of high blood pressure and diabetes can be reduced by the delivery of effective healthcare. Crucially, this entails:

- Partnership between patients and health professionals with the knowledge, ability and resources to take appropriate measures over many years;
- Cheap and effective drugs and the implementation of simple treatment protocols, as promoted by WHO and the CVD initiative of the Global Forum for Health Research.

An appropriate policy strategic framework is essential for such initiatives to be effective on a large scale. Even in the poorest countries people are already seeking healthcare for NCDs in both the public and private sectors, particularly in urban areas. Whatever the balance of priorities between different conditions, existing resources should be used as effectively as possible, Rapid evaluation methods can provide policy-makers with information on the current levels and quality of care and identify the main opportunities for improving health services.

The proper planning and co-ordination of NCD prevention and treatment, whether globally or nationally, requires up-to-date data on risk factor and disease levels—currently missing for much of the world. To address this lack, the WHO Non-Communicable Disease and Mental Health Surveillance section is promoting a standardised approach to enable comparisons across regions and over time, preparing the first ever 'world risk status' report for the major NCDs. This will provide a truly global perspective on the size and nature of the problem.

As this article has shown, NCDs are major health problems even in the world's poorest countries, including those regions where infectious diseases continue to take a huge toll. The NCD burden will grow substantially in low land middle-income countries over the next 10 to 20 years. NCDs will increasingly demand attention and require the right balance between competing priorities for prevention, cure and care. In meeting this challenge, national policy-makers will need to follow the lead of WHO and develop a strategic framework that plans for surveillance, prevention and appropriate health sector reforms.

# 15 City Politics: *A Voice for the Poor*

By 2020 the world's urban population will rise by almost 1.5 billion. Cities and towns house a growing proportion of poor people, partly because of the increased share of urban population of the total but also because economic recession and adjustment policies often hit poorer urban residents the hardest. Cities are associated with economic growth and wealth generation and yet inequality is high. Poor people generally live in substandard conditions, may not benefit from job creation, and suffer high levels of pollution, crime and violence.

How can city governments cope with the challenges of population growth and increased global economic competition, and meet the needs of poor residents/is urban governance responsive to the needs of the poor? Are the agencies responsible for city government, especially the municipalities, addressing poor people's needs? Are NGOs and people's organisations playing a greater role in service delivery? Or is their role one of advocacy and lobbying? If so, how do they relate to the formal political system? Can governments fulfil their responsibilities, including poverty reduction? How can the well-being of poor urban governance institutions priorities their needs? In assessing the responsiveness of city government to poor people, three key questions are addressed:

## How can the Poor Influence the Agenda of the Institutions of Urban Governance?

The influence of poor residents on decision-making is controlled, in part, by the formal political system. Democratisation gives people a vote. However, this vote means more when elected representative depend on the political support of poor people—where they are a majority, or are well organised, or where there is a ward-based system. If poor people are organised enough, to articulate their needs and demand a fair share of urban resources. NGOs can help poor groups organise better and provide support for networking.

Where poor people are not organised it does not mean they are politically powerless. Poor people in this situation, however, are prey to the disadvantages of patronage and unlikely to be included in formal consultative processes. For an electoral system to be truly responsive, specific mechanisms and channels, such as consultative and participatory processes at city an sub-city levels, are needed to complement representative democracy. Athough, these channels do not necessarily include the poorest or make a marked difference to resource allocation, pro-poor decisions are unlikely without them.

## How can Cities Finance their Activities and Reduce Poverty?

Democratisation has not, in many countries brought allocation of financial resources or the revenue-raising capacity for local governments to fulfil their responsibilities. The responsiveness of city governments to poor people's needs thus depends, on whose voices are heard in the arenas of political decision-making. Responsiveness also depends on how available financial resources are allocated and how the programmes they finance are designed. There is scope, for city governments to increase property and business revenues, and to borrow for capital investment. Whether increased financial resources benefit poor people depends on how the demands of external investors and creditors are reconciled with the demands of poor residents; the willingness of politicians and officials to address the distributive implications of existing and planned spending; and efficient transparent financial management. If funds are made available to sub-city levels of government or if expenditure can be influenced by ward councilors, the funds might then be used to meet the priorities of poor residents.

## What are the Necessities of Urban Living and how can Access to then be Ensured?

***An Adequate Income:*** Work opportunities should be the top priority. City governments can, however, support the urban economy in general and the economic activities of the poor in particular. Firstly they can ensure that the basic services are efficiently provided. Secondly city governments can refrain from activities that destroy the assets and livelihoods of the poor, especially eviction of informal settlements and micro-enterprises. Savings and credit schemes can be more appropriately organised at a community level and supported by NGOs.

***Land Ownership*** is a common aspiration for poor households. A home with secure tenure (not necessarily title) provides security, an appreciating asset, access to services, and a base for economic activities. Increasing the opportunities for poor households to gain access to a well-located plot of land is an important component of any poverty reduction strategy. Many never fulfil their dream and the needs of those who cannot, or do not wish to become home owners should not be neglected, however.

Local government is potentially more responsive to poor residents than are central government agencies, although this depends on the balance of political power and bureaucratic perceptions. The limited ability of the public sector to secure benefits for the poor from public-private partnerships in land development, suggest that more informal arrangements and the involvement of CSOs may be better ways forward.

***Environmental Services:*** Land alone will not reduce poverty but must be linked to a healthy living environment—a package of appropriate and affordable environmental services, such as public transport, water and sanitation, solid waste collection, and energy for cooking and lighting. Rather than discussing appropriate standards, detailed issues of financing and affordability or how continued provision can be assured for each of these services, the research focused on how far decision making channels mechanisms and partnership arrangements ensure that providers are responsive to the needs and priorities of poor residents.

Collaborative planning and decision-making arrangements are one promising alternative, despite the current shortcomings of participatory budgeting. For responsiveness to the poor to be built in to such processes, local bureaucrats need to change their attitudes and working practices. Is it possible and acceptable for poor people to have to rely on their own resources their households and networks—resources that are very limited? Informal networks and links can, however, provide mutual support and access to politicians and bureaucrats, community associations thought not always present, inclusive or transparent, can play an important role in articulating poor residents views and in organising self-help activities. There is scope for formal representative community organisations, for informal links between peoples' organsiations and the power structures, and for networking between people's groups. NGOs can play an important role in developing the capacity of community organisations and in facilitating networking. Where NGOs play a role in service delivery. However, there is a danger that the resulting close relationship with local government detracts from their ability to empower poor people and challenge inappropriate policies. City governments, it is clear, cannot cope with the challenges of population and economic growth and respond to the needs of poor people alone. Only in alliance with other actors is there some hope that poverty can be overcome. For CSOs, many of which were forged during struggles for democratisation, this implies moving beyond confrontation to engagement. To form alliances between CSOs and city governments that put the interests of the poor first, poor people must be able to exercise their political rights.

# 16 Rural Poverty in India and Development as a Policy Challenge

Poverty can be overcome, and that the poor can increase their income and production within an appropriate framework. Part of that framework is made up of a flow of resources and local-level institutional development, and there is considerable scope for improvement in both. However, the impact of investment and organisation is strictly determined by the nature of the policy environment. While project and programmes can bring some relief to the rural poor, substantial change needs a strong policy commitment. While the poor can overcome poverty, they will not be able to until this becomes a major focus of national policy and action. In the main, this sort of commitment has not been made in the past—at the expense of both the poor and overall development in many areas.

The current state of India is highly contradictory. On the one hand, there is proclamation of a new order; on the other, increasing value is given to sectional and short-term national and group interests. With an overt concern with the India's poor goes an equal weight given to concern with economic mechanisms and relations that pay little attention to poverty and foster more inequality. The dangers of this situation are real. The lack of concrete attention being given to change will mean greater economic polarisation. Greater polarisation among the better-off, and between the better-off and the poor-means instability and a lack of consensus, a lack of legitimacy.

Poverty is far-reaching, and ought to be curtailed. In a period in which resources everywhere appear restricted, this seems not to be an attractive proposition at the particle level.

Welfare is every where giving way to production as an imperative, just as public expenditure is giving way to private accumulation. Poverty alleviation does not appear to be an ideal whose time has come. The objections are great, but they are also misplaced. Poverty alleviation is not necessarily a drain upon accumulation, and it is not primarily a public activity. Poverty alleviation is primarily the activity of the poor themselves, and their progress necessarily involves productive expansion. If this potential for private expansion has not been realized, it is not because of the nature of the poor, it is because of the way in which national economic affairs have been organized. Economic policy has been oriented towards the better off—not infrequently at the expense of the poor. Given the historic association between wealth and power, the definition of development in terms of the large and the wealthy is hardly surprising.

There is the possibility of associated growth involving both large-scale and small-scale production, the better of and the poor. The realisation of this possibility might result from a new social compact. This social compact is not a commitment to social safety nets and welfare, both of which seem to presuppose that the poor are somehow necessarily out of the growth field. It is a commitment to abolishing artificial and onerous terms of exchange that discriminate against the poor, to investing resources where there are real opportunities for gain, irrespective of whether the economic agents concerned are rich or poor, and to creating the space for the poor to organize to pursue their social and economic interests.

There is a need for a new growth model consistent with new social realities. While the 1980s was a period of clearing away many of the obstacles to development, it was not a period in which there emerged a clear vision of what represented the positive basis for growth, beyond, that is, a general prescription of market-driven operations. The model must pass from admonition to positive prescription to fuel growth by integrating the poor in their rightful place in the production function. It must redefine the position of public expenditure in the development process, and seek to establish market structures which are both equitable and open to the participation of the economically weaker elements of the population. Most of all it must revalue the position and contribution of the poor and small-scale producers in the growth process, particularly in the agricultural sector, but not exclusively agriculture.

This means that the issue is not much one of less government, but of government, both national and local, finding a new rationale for action, including, *inter alia*, creating conditions that will effectively unleash the productive potential of the rural poor.

Financial flows to the poorest Indian are not likely to undergo a very major expansion, especially through private channels. Development will rely very much on the mobilisation of their own resources, and many of these resources are in the hands of the poor, are, indeed, not only the human capital embodied in the poor but also their assets which, while small, individually are cumulatively important in India. The growth model for the 1990s will have to embrace that fact, and build upon it. The paradox of most development models is that they have emphasized the value of what Indians do not have while devaluing what they have: capital intensity has been promoted in situations of scarcity of capital, at the expense of abundant labour and of low-cost methods of manifold increase of the productivity of assets of which the poor do dispose. In a not very indiret way, the creation of poverty has been subsidized. Poverty alleviation is neither a special topic nor a low-cost substitute for growth. Is is neither more nor less "social" than development in general. It is part of the formulation of any sustainable strategy of economic development. In the 1990s it may, and perhaps should, become the dominant issue—not as an alternative to the structural reorganisations of the 1980s, but as a means of filling a growth framework with substance.

# 17 Link Between Disability and Poverty

Disability affects nearly every fifth household in developing countries and is a prevalent contributing factor to family poverty.

An already poor household has an added financial burden when a disabled family member is not involved in productive activities. In the context of extreme poverty, a disability may sometimes turn into an asset when the person uses begging as a way to bolster the family income. But this is a degrading path that does not lead out of poverty.

What aggravates the situation is the fact that poverty is identified as one of the main causes of disability. This is especially so for those at the lowest strata of society who live in precarious conditions without education, hygiene and health care.

An important element of measures aimed at families living in absolute poverty is that they learn how to prevent disability. They must also learn that a disabled family member can take part in economic activities.

Increasing the economic usefulness of a disabled household member can help to reduce the poverty of many families. The income earned by the disabled person not only benefits him or her but the entire household as well.

However, anti-poverty strategies which target disabled household members without attempting to alleviate general household poverty would likely be futile.

One widespread misconception is that disabled people are unable to earn a living and to be self-reliant. As a consequence, disabled people are often targeted only for passives measure of income replacement and social welfare schemes. Active measures of income replacement and social welfare schemes. Active measure in their favour are conceived of as social activities and not economically relevant. Such misconceptions generate and reinforce exclusion, which in turn perpetuates poverty.

This highlights a dimension of poverty often overlooked by economists. They defined poverty only in terms of household income. But poverty also means to lack social status and to lose human dignity.

Thus, a basic criterion for an anti-poverty strategy at the micro-level is whether it serves to establish human dignity. An approach, which merely dishes out state subsidies or international aid to the destitute keeps the recipients in a position of dependence.

Targeting specific groups for poverty alleviation measures is always a highly sensitive issue. It can damage the fragile social fabric and may result in greater poverty for some while favouring others. Such a risk may be avoided through a participatory approach, which actively involves the poor and assists them in their efforts to gain control over their lives.

Disabled people are more likely to be poorer than their non-disabled peers because of the discrimination, which accompanies disability, not because of the impairment itself.

They suffer from social exclusion and frequently find themselves trapped in a web of neglect. The problem is even more acute for disabled women, who encounter enormous prejudices and obstacles in their quest to participate in social and economic life.

A more enlightened society will seek to integrate disabled people, to give them opportunities to learn and to work as others do. It will adjust the physical environment to accommodate their special needs.

This planet belongs to all people. If some people are trapped somewhere, we must all come forward to remove the causes of their discomfort. At the same time we must leave our shores open for anybody who decides to join us, or any body who decides to part our company.

Poverty denies a person control over his destiny. Poverty means not being able to tell what tommorrow would be like. If we examine the situation carefully we will see that the poverty is neighter created by the poor, nor sustained by the poor. It is the system of policies and institutions that we have built around us that creates and sustains poverty. Poverty is the denial of human rights. Over one billion people live below the absolute poverty line right now on this planet are denied of almost all human rights. There is no way one can defend the existence of poverty anywhere. Poverty is a disgrace for the entire man—kind Because we allow another humanbeing to die of hunger, or malnutrition, or common curable diseases, or exposure to climate, we are reduced to less humanbeings. If a particular world system is responsible for creating this massive poverty we must act to replace it.

Resource-wise or technology-wise, there is no reason why poverty should exist and continue to deepen and widen. If we make up our minds to wipe out poverty from the surface of the earth, the worst aspect of poverty can be removed within the next couple of decades.

Each humanbeing is a wonderful creation of the creator. Each humabeing is born with great potentials. Poverty denies any opportunity for a person to achieve any of his/her potential. We have built a world system which is in the habit of pushing people down not building them up. It creates barriers around individuals, rather than remove them.

The most effective step that we must take to remove poverty is to create a system which creates enabling conditions for people and removes the existing barriers. The institutional barriers were skillfully crafted over the centuries to benefit a handful of people.

Resource-poor nations with high incidence of poverty waste away enormous human capability each day by denying poor people the use of their energy and ingenuity. If they could have been made economically active, not only they could have contributed in the national production, they would have helped expand the domestic market for the products produced. The disabled one can be transformed into the engine of grwoth if we only allow them to unleash their capacity.

We cannot be at peace with ourselves if we know there is a human being who lives a life worse than an animal. A humanbeing is supposed to live differently than an animal. He/She is supposed to live a life with human dignity. Human dignity is what distinguishes a human being from an animal. When we cannot ensure this dignity for others, our own dignity becomes an empty pretense.

There must be a thousand and one ways to remove poverty from the earth. We may or may not know some of those ways already. Obviously there are many more ways yet to be designed, each more effectively than others. When we shall find them, how many of them we shall find, how quickly we find them will depend on how eager we are to find them. But to say that poverty cannot be overcome, directly and quickly, is to underestimate the capacity of human mind.

# 18 Women and Poverty

It is becoming more evident that the majority of tne poor in developed and developing worlds are women. Poverty among rural women is growing faster than among rural men. Over the past 20 years, for example, the number of women in absolute poverty rose by 50 per cent as against some 30 per cent for rural men. The alarming evidence concerning the underlying trends for this process strongly indicates that the gender composition of the poor is veering towards a greater share of women.

Poverty manifests itself in many ways among migrant and refugee women, elderly women and children and indigenous women. Poverty is a complex, diverse and dynamic condition stemming out of depravation with respect to income, from social inferiority, isolation, physical weakness, powerlessness and humiliation.

Analysis of women's poverty suggest that its main causes stem from the perpetual disadvantage of women in terms of their position in the labour market, access to productive resources and income for the satisfaction of their basic needs. They also demonstrate that poor women possess exceptional resourcefulness, initiative and entrepreneurial spirit and that they show tenacity and self-sacrifice in trying to take a long-term view of their poor economic conditions and in safeguarding their livelihoods.

Development is the most important challenge facing the human race. The lack of progress in the last twenty years in the eradication of poverty and growing proportion of women among the poor is the single most important threat to the progress of development and its sustainability. As long as three-quarters of the world population continue to suffer from acute depravation, as long as profound imbalances in global consumption continue to persist, and more important, as long as the spread of poverty, particularly among women, continues unchecked, there can be no development. The history of the development process shows again that the economic status of women is the key variable in the solution to the poverty crisis. It is time for the full recognition of the fact that women are part of the solution to poverty, and to the stagnating development, not part of the problem.

The Earth Summit in Rio, the Human Rights Conference in Vienna, the Population Conference in Cairo and the Beijing Conference all were milestone events in terms of advancing our understanding of the crucial role of women in development and focusing the attention of the international community on the issues concerning the role of women in the work place and in society. All of them drew attention to women's full and effective participation in development. None, however, full articulated how to achieve this challenging task.

It is important to retain focus on the issue of economic potential when discussing poverty among women because it is clear that power is only meaning something in practical terms if it is reinforced by economic power. Women have the means to transform productive resources into such power if only enabling environment is created. It is not the lack of capabilities, but that of resources, which is clearly responsible for women's poverty.

Sometimes the so badly needed resources are not even truly scarce. Billions have been wasted on arms purchases around the globe and particularly in the countries, which can not afford such misallocation of public funds. At the same time, wome's organisations from grassroots to the international level are poorly funded. Such misallocation of resources at the time when poverty among women is increasing, is immoral and unacceptable, not only on the part of the governments which pursue such wasteful policies, but also on the part of the suppliers, who in most cases are developed economies.

Government's responsibilities do not end here. It is extremely important, and indeed it is the main duty of every government around the world, to provide a conducive environment for economic growth and stability by pursuing responsible and sound macro-economic policies, which will enable the economy to grow without marginalizing women. When inflation is rampant, when political climate is unstable leading to conflicts and civil strife, little can be done for poverty alleviation.

# 19 Taking a Lead in the Fight Against Poverty?

## World Bank and IMF Speed Implementation of their New Strategy

A change in development policy strategy in the poorest countries is at present being prepared with incredible speed. The IMF-style structural adjustment programmes that have been criticised for many years are being scrapped. The countries are now to take their own decisions on their paths to development. Their governments will no longer formulate poverty reduction programmes top-down, but in an intensive and long-term dialogue with societal groups and organisations. Governments and institutions of the North commit themselves to supporting these processes, such as by debt relief on an unprecedented scale. Dream or reality?

## New Strategy Paper

Behind this euphoria lines a new abbreviation, PRSP, standing for Poverty Reduction Strategy Paper, which the IMF and World Bank invented last year. The G-7 countries in Cologne not only announced debt relief for the heavily indebted poor countries (HIPCs) but also demanded that it must serve above all for poverty reduction. The PRSP concept was then presented at the annual conference of the two Bretton Woods organisations.

The most important principles of the new "super weapon" in the fight against poverty are:

- PRSPs are papers, which describe the medium-term development paths of the poorest countries of the

South, particularly their strategies to combat poverty, and by this means enlist international support. A PRSP is not only the prerequisite for granting debt forgiveness in the context of the HIPC initiative. It is also necessary for all new IMF and World Bank loans to the so-called IDA countries, the some 70 poorest countries that receive concessional loans from the World Bank's International Development Agency (IDA). According to the World Bank, PRSPs should also be required for all future pledges of bilateral development assistance.

- Not only social sector programmes, but also the economic and financial policies of the developing countries are in future to be aimed at fighting poverty. Previously, the IMF always pronounced that a growth-oriented national economy and a far-reaching integration in the world market would have a trickle-down effect and also benefit the poor. Now the poor are to be asked what policies can help materially to improve their situation.
- PRSPs are to be developed on the basis of self-responsible country ownership. Accordingly, development and structural adjustment strategies are no longer to be developed by the Washington finance institutions, but the countries themselves.
- The heading "country ownership" is to underline that not only governments are called upon, PRSPs should come into being in a participatory process. That means involvement of trade unions, NGOs cooperatives, associations, grassroots groups, political parties and parliaments. A country's PRSP should be developed in a societal debate, a dialogue between governments on one side and parliamentary, private sector and civil society on the other.

## Rhetoric or Reality?

Are PRSPs the expression of a change of paradigm? In brief, if all what the papers contain is implemented in a consistent and wide-ranging, way, the chances of achieving it are good but there are a number of open questions. The answers to them will have a bearing on success or failure.

Is the IMF really changing its policy on the poorest countries or merely wrapping its old policy in new words? The growing criticise of the IMF in recent years strengthened latterly by the evaluation of the ESAF (Enhanced Structural Adjustment Facility) programmes, which once again proved their blatant weaknesses called for reaction and is now triggeringchanges – real or only rhetorical? There will be no more old-style ESAF loans based on macro-economic structural adjustment programmes. But the credit line remains, and is now called the Poverty Reduction and Growth Facility (PRGF). This will be granted on the basis of the PRSPs, which in each case must also be accepted by the IMF board of directors. How much influence will the IMF have on the design of the PRSPs? What happens if a government choose macro-economic strategies combat poverty which go against previous IMF policy? Open questions. Moreover, there is still no answer to the question of why the IMF is at al coming on with long-term and low-interest lines of credit in the poorest countries.

## Mixed Feelings with Regard to World Bank Role

- Will the World Bank use the PRSP process to expand its own institutional power further? NGOs in the North and South are viewing this with mixed feelings. Many welcome the fact that for the moment the World Bank appears to be asserting itself against its twin, the IMF. On the other hand, 50 years of experience with World Bank strategies have certainly not strengthened their trust in the Bank's ability to make a convincing fight against poverty. That is why the EURODAD network also questions the role of the World Bank (and the IMF) in the PRSP process. It says the papers should not be presented to the two financial institutions, whose power over the development strategies of countries of the South thus would increase further. Rather, PRSPs should for example, be laid before a Round Table of all donors chaired by the United Nations Development Programme (UNDP).

## Ownership

- The principles of developing countries being responsible for their own development strategies are as old as it is—in theory—right. There have been frequent complaints about shortcomings in ownership. But now, after decades of development strategies being set and structural adjustment programmes being dictated from outside, the governments of the poorest countries, which in many cases have only weak institutional capacities, can hardly taken on sole respnsibility overnight. In addition, of course, not a few of the countries are ruled by corrupt political elites (promoted from outside over decades) that give little reason to hope they would immediately switch to poverty reduction polities. Scepticism and critical observation is justified even if there is no alternative to governments of the south taking over greater responsibility.
- Civil society actors are now asked to help out in particular in those countries whose governments appear to be less trustwothy. A nice idea that has little to do with real life. Civil society actors in developing countries in general and in the poorest countries in particular are extraordinarily weak institutions which in many cases are totally dependent on financing from the North.
- The civil society landscape in other countries is even weaker. However, social actors in many countries could make useful contributions to developing sustainable strategies. But that calls for meaningful and lasting support, including financial support, capacity-building, and in some countries also political pressure to gain scope for societal engagement.

It is reasonable that not only the World Bank and other official donors but also, and above all, the northern NGO partners of these actors are now giving much thought to how civil societies in the south can be strengthened.

## Participation?

Even assuming there were civil society actors capable of dialogue, that does not clarify what participation in the PRSP process is really supposed to mean. Is civil society only to be listened to, or can it if necessary refuse to approve a PRSP? What impact would have on acceptance of the document by the IMF and World Bank and other donor? And in view of the great time pressure, will civil society be at all able to formulate discuss and feed their positions into the process? It could be of decisive importance for the current debate on the PRSP model to delink the urgently needed debt relief from drawing up a PRSP programme, which simply needs more time. For example, it is conceivable that there would be no great problems in granting a country a moratorium on debt servicing so long as a PRSP process is continuing and then for giving debt when it is completed. That would ease the time problem for NGOs and at the same time maintain pressure on governments actually to arrive at poverty reduction strategies that were developed in a participatory process.

## Other Causes of Poverty in Developing Countries

The entire current process is focused on the countries of the south, their governments and societies. That diverts attention from the responsibility of the donors and creditors. Not only that the IMF's structural adjustment programmes to date have been counterproductive for fighting poverty (why does the IMF not admit that openly just for Once?) Not only that the now promised debt reliefs are coming much too late the debt crisis of the poorest countries was deplored decades ago!). The present strategy also ignore various other exogenous causes of poverty in the South. What impacts do the finance and trade policies of northern countries have on the modest attempts to enable sustainable development in the South? What consequences will the continuing cutting of development budgets have on the South (no one anyway ventures to talk nowadays about the old 0.7 per cent ODA-GNP ratio) Fort the donors and creditors to now pass the buck of sole responsibility to the governments of the South and present themselves in the background as noble do-gooders may be a successful strategy in terms of domestic politics, but not an acceptable one for development policy.

# 20 The Dematerialisation of the World Economy

The first Industrial Revolution marked the transition from robber-and-plunder colonialism to the systematic development of the "overseas" territories in the framework of an international division of labour between raw materials suppliers and manufacturers of finished goods. There was an "historic integration" of the colonised areas in the development of their parent-states. What will the third Industrial Revolution do for the Third World ? Will it now come to an "historic separation" ?

The end of the East-West conflict was reason enough to talk about a radical change in world politics. But at the same time an upheaval in the world economy is taking place that possibly will have even wider impacts. As a reference point for the following thoughts, three dimensions of this change are pointed out:

1 The upgrading of processing information rather than materials as object of economic activity (technological dimension);

2 the evolvement of global communications networks (socio-cultural dimension);

3 the change of the nature of work (socio-economic dimension).

All three dimensions can be summarised under the buzzphrase "tertialisation of the world economy."

In that respect, talk of the "Third Industrial Revolution" is misleading. It is not about a third epoch of industrialisation, but about the beginning of a de-industrialisation, the transition from the industrial to the information society.

## Historic Separation ?

In the 1960s and early 1970s, there was often talk of the Third World as the Third Sector of the world economy. Also then the Third World was not much more than an "imaginary community". But as such it had a certain significance in world politics. This implied not only its strategic role in the East-West conflict and its ideological function as the supporter of different "third paths" between capitalism and socialism. It was also about the Third World's attested "chaos power". That linked the fear (in the North) and the hope (in the South) that the developing countries would be in a position to cut off the industrial nations from supplies of important raw materials, thus putting them under pressure. But it was soon seen that both sides had over estimated this possibility, even with regard to oil. Instead of supply bottlenecks arising, raw materials prices plummeted. For some commodities, the fall in prices exceeded those of the great Depression of 1929-30.

This was due, inter alia, to the conjunction of lower demand from the industrial nations and expansion of production by the raw materials suppliers. Business activities dependent upon the supply of raw materials are tending to lose importance compared with the overall development of the global economy. The reason for this is to be seen in the transition from a material to an information economy.

This transition is taking place in line with the revolutionizing of data transmission and the expansion of financial transactions which are not directly related to changes in the production of materials. The speed of the changes is remarkable.

However, the dematerialisation of business activities does not lead to decoupling of the Third World from the world economy. Declining market shares in world trade are not the expression of separation, but a loss of the affected countries positions in the world economy. Thus, the impact of dematerialisation is "only" that the negotiating positions of raw materials suppliers vis-a-vis the industrial nations will deteriorate further.

## Differentiation of the Third World

But the radical change in the global economy is affecting some developing countries worse than others. Sub-saharan Africa, and some countries in West and South Asia and Latin America are being pushed back further. The oil-producing countries with their high per capita export earnings will be able to hold their positions in the world economy for some time to come. The threshold countries of East and South-East Asia can expand theirs so long as they can continue to attract a growing share of global industrial production, and at the same time participate in the tertialisation of the world economy in the shape of rapidly-growing financial transactions. Thereby it should be noted that the degree of tertialisation in itself is not an adequate indicator for economic avant-gardism. Brazil exhibits a high degree of tertialisation in combination with a low macro-economic development dynamics. A good part of its tertialisation is being achieved by speculative financial transactions with their inherently greater risks and uncertainties that in the industrial countries. Such dangers have been demonstrated by Mexico's peso crisis and its repercussions on the whole of Latin America.

In some Third World countries, a "location annuity" has replaced the old raw materials one. Here it's about providing locations for off-shore transactions which offer international capital traders a maximum of freedom of movement combined with low taxation. Suitable for such operations are small countries which, despite low levy rates, achieve significant income in macro-economic terms.

The radical changes in the world economy are spurring the differentiation of the Third World Without, however, necessarily fostering a dissolution of the Third World as an "imaginary community". It is precisely the advanced countries of East and South-East Asia that are showing a certain interest in the formulation of joint positions of the "South" in order to secure their own positional gains in the global economy. It's not by chance that the non-aligned countries and the Group of 77 have formed a joint coordination committee, and that the ASEAN countries are changing course on the international human rights policy.

Hitherto, the developing countries' strategy was to broaden the concept of human rights as a justification for demands on the industrial nations. But of late some developing countries, led by the ASEAN states, have questioned the universal validity of human rights even after their universality was confirmed by consensus at the Conference on Human Rights in Vienna in 1993. Playing a role in this policy is the governments' fear that due to the expansion of global communications networks, the behaviour patterns and preferences of their own people could in some way become similar to those of the West. As the rulers see it, that would be detrimental to the continuation of the development models practised so far.

## Internet Creates New Cultural Dimension

Much information which Asian governments view as subversive in already globally available on the Internet. The old struggle over the world information order, which at first was primarily a clinch between East and West, is thus taking on a new dimension. For with the growing importance of computer literacy to a country's ability to assert itself on world markets, the Asian threshold countries have not only an interest in controlling the on-line communication but also to expand it and the know–how that it requires.

Even the critics of any interventions in the internet and other global communications networks must admit that modern communications technologies are politically blind and their use in itself does not represent progress. The setting up and expansion of global information highways will offer forum not only to people who want to use it for education and enlightenment, but also to all shades of fundamentalists. These highways will not necessarily bring the misery of many Third World regions closer to the industrial countries, but possibly rather strengthen the tendency to process all world events as entertainment.

## Global Two-thirds Society

The gravest aspect of the current upheaval in the world economy is its negative impact on jobs. The information economy needs for fewer workers than an economy based on materials. Instead, the demands on the skills of the workers are growing. Twenty per cent of the world workforce will in future be employed as (overworked) "intelligence workers". Eighty per cent will work part-time, if they are not underemployed or jobless. So the tertialisation of the global economy delivers more underemployment rather than more leisure time. The workers who are rationalised out of their jobs in the industrial sector cannot be absorbed by the service sector because it, too, is not left untouched by rationalisation measures. The civil service is also cutting back on staff. At all levels, there's a race to make the greatest possible savings on payrolls. At the same time, there's growing pressure to cut costs in providing for the victims of this development. That means thinning out the social security safety net.

The bottom line is that the two-thirds society, which developmentaql action groups hitherto assumed was limited to the Third World, is spreading worldwide. That, however, will not in the foreseeable future lead to an amendment of the North-South disparities. It's true that the change in the global economy is taking place faster and to a greater extent in the industrial nations. But rationalisation is also happening in the developing countries in a bid to boost their competitiveness. So the upheaval in the world economy aggravates the problems which exist in a majority of the developing countries, while creating new ones in the industrial nations. The need for action on the North-South policy is growing, while the industrial nations. The need for action on the North-South Policy is growing, while the industrial nations' scope for concessions and compromises is shrinking. The new social question which is now crystallizing at global level is not being answered. The consequences are unforeseeable.

## Another Loser ?

It's more probable that a sharpening of the North-South confrontation is to be reckoned with. For the industrial nations will attempt to keep the social costs of the information economy at bay for as long as possible. The trade unions will thereby compete with the developing countries for jobs for their memebers. But this policy has its limits precisely because of the peaking of the problems in the industrial nations. Overstepping these limits means war, and passively accepting them chaos and social decay. Solutions could be sought in two directions: effective taxation of the information economies, and the creation of jobsin the non-profit sector. But it's possible there are no global solutions for global problems. That would mean for at least part of the Third World a renewal of the old debate on partial decoupling from the world economy.

# 21 Solving the Unemployment Problem by Looking Beyond the Job

If you had a job, you worked; if you didn't, you didn't. Having a job meant being employed by an organisation in a clearly defined and stable occupational role, with duties, hours, rates of pay and promotion all more or less standardized. But the job—in that meaning of the world—is a social invention, and a fairly recent one.

The job—the kind that you had, or hoped to get—became a central fixture of life. Its importance was great because it served many needs: For managers and efficiency experts, job assignments were the key to assembly-line manufacturing. For union organizers, jobs protected the rights of workers. For political reformers, standardized civil service positions were the essence of good government. Jobs provided an identify to immigrants and recently, urbanized farm workers. They provided a sense of security for individuals and an organizing principle for society.

Jobs functioned in so many ways that it is surprising how many organisations are now opting for other ways to define and manage work. The second job shift is underway. Its emergence can be seen in the increasing use of temporary and part-time workers and contracted-out services, the changing relationships between workers and management, the growing popularity of self-employment and small business. Indeed, "de-jobbing" is proceeding at such a pace that many economists, management experts and futurists are now talking freely about the end of the job. Bridges predicts that the job as we now know it will disappear entirely—replaced by new kinds of flexible work assignments in post-job organisations—and be remembered only as a quaint artifact of the industrial age.

One reason for the change in work is the economic rules of the survival game among organisations that employ workers. To stay successful in today's hitech consumer economy, businesses have had to re-model themselves into what some experts call "agile companies"—ones that are able to respond quickly to conditions in ever-changing fragmenting, competitive markets.

The "knowledge worker", whose work involves not simply doing something, but also applying theoretical or analytical skills. Such workers are replacing the industrial labourer as the dominant part of the workforce—and their productive activities are likely to be organized and structured much differently from those of their assembly-line predecessors.

De-jobbing as a result of new technology or the emergence of a service economy is a phenomenon that gets a lot of attention these days; but it is not the whole story. At all levels of society, people are improvising livelihoods that do not fit the industrial-era model. Immigrants to the developed countries, often unable to find steady jobs, nevertheless find places in the new landscape by being mobile, flexible, resourceful and imaginative; they moonlight, work, part-time, share jobs, start small businesses. Their lives are often extremely difficult, but they are also instructive to those of us believe you either have a job or you're out of luck.

It is too early to evaluate the implications of this multifaceted transformation of work, or to dismiss it as simply good or bad. Nevertheless, one cannot deny that it is taking place, and will bring about dramatic social changes.

On the downside, the job shift is causing great hardships for many workers and their families. It poses serious challenges to policy-makers, political activists and labour leaders. The basic question appears to be whether the key to global employment-development strategy is to play "catch-up"—trying to bring millions of people around the world into jobs in industries and the public sector; or to play "leapfrog"-creating new forms of employment.

The proposal to generate more employment in agriculture, for example, is based on new demand for agricultural exports from developing countries. The policies designed to make the most of this opportunity include measures to upgrade technology, raise productivity, ensure the supply of essential inputs, establish marketing and distribution channels, create links between agriculture and industry, and cater to export markets.

The issue of part-time work, another kind of employment that is seriously undervalued in the traditional industrial era job mind-set. Part-time work may not offer much at this point to developing countries, where many people are under employed and wages are low, but it can be of great help in more advanced economies. And it is likely to be a big part of the global work picture in the years ahead.

A certain agility may also be necessary in agriculture, particularly in countries that for many years have depended heavily on producing commodities such as sugar for export as a means of generating income and employment. As Northern laboratories develop non-agricultural substitutes for many of these commodities—and this is already beginning to happen—the bottom may fall out of "monoculture" economies, only economic, but will have long-run political implications as communities attempt to reorganize themselves in response to the changed conditions. It is, therefore, in the interest of raw materials exporters to closely monitor current trends in biotechnology and the use of genetic resources and modify their internal policies in anticipation of potential long-term effects."

This calls for flexibility, and an ability to get information and to act on it. Government officials, development workers, community leaders and individuals will, in some respects, all have to be "knowledge workers" if they are to keep ahead of global changes. Jobs are going to be created not just by putting people to work, but by finding-or creating-new niches where they can be productive.

It is still possible to talk about jobs for all, and to resist the assumption made by many economists that high levels of unemployment are now inevitable. But, as we move ahead into the global information economy, we may be moving back into an older conception of the job, and seeing it again as something you do, rather than as something you have—or that has you.

# 22 Income Gap Widens

The gap in income among the people of the world has been widening. In 1960, according to United Nations statisticians, the richest 20 per cent of the world's people received 30 times more income than the poorest 20 per cent. By 1991, they were getting 61 times more. While the poorest one-fifth in 1960 received a meagre 2.3 per cent of world income, by 1991 that revenue share had fallen to 1.4 per cent. The income share of the richest fifth, meanwhile, rose from 70 per cent to 85 per cent.

These disparities prevail both among countries and within them, and the large gap between individuals world wide reflects the combination of both of those splits. Almost four fifths of all people live in the developing world, where incomes are only fraction of those in industrial countries. In turn, within countries in both categories, gaps in income between citizens can be even wider.

The widest income gap reported within a country is in Botswana, where during the 1980s the richest 20 per cent of society received over 47 times more income than the poorest 20 per cent. Brazil was second, with a ratio of 32 to 1. In Guatemala and Panama, the ratio stood at 30 to 1.

The rapidly growing economies of East Asia have had income patterns similar to those of Western Europe and North America, with the richest one-fifth often earning 5 to 10 times more than the poorest fifth. In South Asia, India, Bangladesh, and Pakistan have had relatively even distributions of income, with the richest 20 per cent getting only four to five times more than the poorest guintile. Some countries that have had military conflicts apparently based in part on inequities among citizens, never the less have relatively even income distributions.

The split between countries and people can be seen in the marketplace. The value of luxury goods sales world-wide—high-fashion clothing and top-of-the-line autos, for example—exceeds the gross national products of two-thirds of the world-s countries. The world's average income, roughly $4,000 a year, is well below the US poverty line.

The poorest fifth of the world accounted for 0.9 per cent of world trade, 1.1 per cent of global domestic investment, 0.9 per cent of global domestic savings, and just 0.2 per cent of global commercial credit at the beginning of the 1990s. Each of those shares declined between 1960 and 1990.

These disparities are reflected in the consumption of many resources. At the start of this decade, industrial countries home to roughly a fifth of the world's population, accounted for about 86 per cent of the consumption of aluminium, and chemicals, 81 per cent of the paper, 80 per cent of the iron and steel, and three-quarters of the timber and energy. Since then, economic growth in developing countries has probably reduced these percentages. China's economy, for example, is more than 50 per cent larger now than it was in 1990, and developing countries have passed industrial ones in fertilizer consumption.

Uneven income distribution is shaping some of the most important trends in the world today. It raises crime rates, for example. And it drives migration. People have long responded to economic disparities by following a path from poor regions to richer ones, as tens of millions of workers chase higher wages and better opportunities. Some 1.6 million Asians and Middle Easterners were working in Kuwait and Saudi Arabia before they fled war in 1991, and at least 2.5 million Mexicans live in the United States.

The same is true within countries: rising disparities of income are adding to the growth of cities through rural to urban migration. Latin America, with some of the highest disparities of income among its citizens, is also the most urbanized region of the developing world—not entirely by coincidence. Since 1950, city dwellers there have risen from 42 per cent of the population to 73 per cent.

For many years, China had one of the most equal distributions of income in the world. But now that is changing, as income in its southern provinces and special economic zones soar while those in rural areas rise much more slowly. Also not coincidentally, the Chinese National Academy of Social Sciences forecasts that by 2010, half the population will live in cities, compared with 28 per cent today and only 10 per cent in the early 1980s.

In the early 1990s, developing world economies, especially, in East Asia, have grown faster than the economies of the industrial countries. This has the potential to shrink disparities of income, if poorer countries continue to catch up. Yet even if the gaps among countries narrow, the gaps between people may not, because economic growth is distributed so unevenly within nations. Despite the recent restoration of economic growth in Latin America, no progress is expected in reducing poverty, which is even likely to increase slightly.

Meanwhile, in some regions almost no one has been getting richer. The per capita income of most sub Saharan African nations actually fell during the 1980's. In sub-Sahaan Africa, the poorest geographic region, an estimated one-third of all a college graduates have left the continent. That loss of talented people, due in large part to poverty and a lack of opportunities in Africa, will make it even more difficult for the continent to advance.

The economic growth that has the potential to close income gaps among people in the developing world is instead become a splitting off, with some parts of societies joining the industrial world while others remain behind. Singapore, Hongkong, and Taiwan have begun to look like wealthy industrial countries, for example. Now parts of China are following, as are the wealthier segments of Latin American society and of Southeast Asian countries. This is good news for members of the middle-income countries and for the world. But it may do little to help the poorest fifth of humanity.

# 23 Employment and Promoting Ecology: *How a Service Culture Could Put People Back to Work*

We are facing two big and urgent social problems: employment and ecology. Both the unemployment of millions of people and the progressive destruction of the ecosphere are alarming. But they are linked with each other. The 'greening' of industrial products, processes and services could provide many more jobs.

Unemployment has many causes, including:

- Sluggish markets;
- Stagnating or declining purchasing power;
- Growing uncertainty about the future at all levels;
- lack of will and/or ability to innovate.

But joblessness is by far due mostly to the high efficiency of industrial machinery, which produces ever more, ever faster, with ever fewer workers.

## Waste of Resources

The extremely high productive use of human labour and the extremely low productive use of resources are manifested by gigantic mountains of waste. Already today, the junked cars on scrap heaps alone would form a line that would reach to the moon. The scene is the same with discarded electrical and electronic appliances. Every year, millions of tons of ovens, washing machines, refrigerators, dishwashers, TV sets, entertainment electronics equipment and small appliances are being wasted.

If we throw away all these things after a relatively short time we are not only being wasteful and irresponsible with resources, but equally so with people's work. For with the products and materials we discard, we also dispose of the human labour they contain. It is imperative that we radically reduce the enormous turnovers of material and energy. In other words, the productivity of raw materials and energy must be markedly increased. Specifically, that means we must draw as many services as possible from one kilogram of material or 1 kWh of energy. Reducing the enormous flows of materials into the industrial system, as well as developing cycles of materials and responsibility (the manufacturer taken back and repairing and/or remanufacturing used products and materials) and the main pillars of a sustainable development that can cope with the future.

The industrialized nations must cut their consumption of raw materials by a factor of about 10 by 2050; if they are to be able to handle the challenges of the future. To achieve that reduction, innovation efforts must be directed at increasing resource productivity and/or ecological efficiency. In particular, strategies to extend the useful life of goods and intensify their use could result in reducing both the speed and volume of the flows of resources to industry.

## Increasing Resource Productivity

In dealing with nature, we and industry are facing radical change. This is the transition from environmental protection (preservation of nature and health) to greater resource productivity (which at the same time means greater competitiveness). As a rule, environmental protection costs money, while higher resource productivity usually cuts manufacturing costs and/or increases a company's profitability. If the company can sell the same utility or benefits while using fewer resources, it saves twofold: in buying raw materials and on waste disposal. Thereby the rule is that goods and components cycles are more profitable than resources cycles, and that the company which is first in the market gains an additional competitive advantage in terms of a lead in knowledge and image.

If a service, or benefits in the form of services, can be sold instead of products, the decoupling of company success and materials flows is even greater.

**Impacts on Employment**

The two social problem areas of work and ecology have to date been perceived and treated separately in politics, in industry and in our own minds. And, I believe, with little result. The link between the two must be established.

The strategies to boost resource productivity would have considerable impacts on the change in industrial structures, on handling existing product inventories, and on employment. In particular, the strategies would lead to a switch of focal point from a raw materials-intensive and use-value-related service economy. This is where another view of profitability comes in. Business management would no longer focus on value added, but on maintenance of value over longer periods based on the intrinsic value of a product. Expressed as a question, the value factor, which would move to the centre of business thinking and dealing, means: how can the utilisation value be improved and sold? How can products be made with as few raw materials and as little energy as possible and create a high benefit as pollutant-free as possible for as long as possible during their entire life-cycle?

With regard to employment, the production of long-life goods would appear at first sight to lead to a reduction in the need for work. In fact, however, the strategies to increase resources productivity have positive net employment impacts. The reason is that saving resources is based in principle on substituting energy by work, rather than the reverse as has been customary to date.

If the useful life of products is extended, that will not only preserve most of the materials and energy they contain as well as the work invested in them. The products will also require a considerable amount of mostly skilled work input. Reconditioning products is as a rule more labour-intensive than manufacturing them. So large-scale reconditioning and repair work increase the number of skilled jobs and at the same time reduces the inflows of materials and energy.

Comparing a car with a life-cycle of 20 years with two others that each have useful lives of 10 years gives a good example. The first car causes an increase in employment per life-year of about 50 per cent in terms of total work input in manufacture, service, repairs and reconditioning while at the same time reducing the energy consumption by half.

## Regionalisation of Industry

Extending product service life would also mean replacing energy and/or capital by skilled work, helping to save money to boot. But not only rising costs of disposal, materials and energy would reduce consumption. Increasing transport costs would also mean that carrying all kinds of freight halfway around the world would make less and less business sense. That would result in ever more products and materials being circulated, reconditioned, and recycled or reduced on a regional basis. In turn, that would create regional jobs, and be more profitable as well as more productive of technology—not only from ecological aspects.

In addition, a way of doing business which encompassed material and responsibility cycles would no longer differentiate between manufacturing and reconditioning, or between marketing and remarketing. The structure of such an economy would be predominantly decentralised and regionalised so that it could adapt itself to the new cycles. It also would benefit from the greater efficiency of the new working practices.

True, jobs would be lost in the sectors of central production, and raw materials extraction and processing. But at the same time, more and higher-skilled jobs would emerge. These would not only be better qualified jobs, but also decentralized because reconditioning, repairs and maintenance must be done near the customer. And that, in turn, would also reduce goods traffic.

In addition, skilled workers would be needed because in many cases of small production runs it makes sense and is also more economical to hire such people. They can work faster and more flexibly and mostly cheaper than fully automated production lines.

There also would be a growing need for maintenance, repairs and reconditioning. More and more people would be wanted for reconditioning, that is, the remanufacturing of old products. As reconditioning involves far more craft work than highly rationalised new production, there would be a positive impact on the labour market if there were more of the former and correspondingly less of the latter.

## From Production to Services

Switching to long-life products and changing from selling products to selling use-values would strengthen the current trend of jobs shifting from industrial production to the service sector. For example, if the service of individual transport were to be sold instead of the product car, the company with the competitive advantage would be the one that had a service centre in every town and village, with appropriately staffed workshops and sales or rental facilities.

Enduring change towards a knowledge-intensive and use-value-related service economy would not only mean that more people would be needed to fill jobs. It would offer more opportunities for part-time work, as well as possibilities of employment for older people and the handicapped. People who earlier could not keep up with the pace of working life would be more inclined to return to it. Another impact would be that many companies would reduce their dependence on the world market. They would no longer switch certain tasks abroad, but assign them to their part-time employees, helping them to meet their commitments as self-employed entrepreneurs.

The latter would be accommodated by an ecology-driven fiscal reform which would make massive cuts or changes in subsidies and raise the cost of energy and raw materials consumption. This move would be accompanied by a reduction in income tax and non-wage costs such as social security contributions. The market would thus be more efficient, energy– and material-intensive new production more expensive, labour intensive repair work and reconditioning cheaper, and jobs would remain in the home country or region.

A number of more recent studies show clearly that an ecological tax reform would help to create jobs, and thereby could make a decisive contribution to reducing unemployment.

# 24 Consuming the Future

Now that we are to reach six billion of us, it is a good point to check again on what sort of lifestyles we pursue and what is the environmental impact of those lifestyles. It is curious that we have spent several decades being concerned about the growing numbers of humankind while not giving at least an equal amount of attention to the levels of living we aspire to, and how many natural resources we chew up thereby and how much population and waste we cause.

Everybody is a consumer of sorts. True, every fifth person scarcely qualifies for that designation, consuming goods worth less than $1 per day. Conversely, every seventh person qualifies for a designation of super-consumer, with a cash income at least fifty times greater. These latter are the people who, through their carbon dioxide emissions, are disrupting everybody's climate dozens of times more than the average citizen of the One Earth. Fair Play, anyone?

Much as the have-nots seek to match the have's, it is plain their efforts will not work out for a long time to come, at best. If every Chinese person were to consume just one additional chicken per year and if the said chicken were to be raised primarily on grain, this would account for as much grain per year as all the grain exports of the number two exporter, Canada. If the Chinese were to raise their per-capita consumption of beef, now only 4 kgs per year, to that of Americans, 45 kg, and if the additional beef were produced largely in feedlots after the manner of the United States, it would account for as much extra grain as the entire US grain harvest, less than one-third of which is exported. Because of its recent climbing up the food chain toward a meat-based diet, China has become one of the world's leading importers of grain. The global grain market today is around 200 million tons per year, and shows scant scope for significant increase.

As a further measure of its ambitions, the Chinese government has designated the auto industry as one of five industry "pillars". Today China has fewer cars than Los Angeles. If per-capita car ownership, together with oil consumption, were to match that of the United States; China would need 80 million barrels of oil per day—by contrast with the world's 1996 oil output of 64 million barrels of oil per day. The surge in carbon dioxide emissions would be unprecedented.

All this notwithstanding, there are already some 250 million newly affluent people in China. They are people with a household income equivalent to perhaps US$20,000, and enough discretionary income to enjoy the perquisites of the good life as perceived by these nouveaux riches. Top of the shopping lists are meat and more meat, followed by cars whether big or small. These are the badges of success: they show you have Arrived.

The new consumers in China are matched by at least 200 million in India, and tens of millions in South Korea, Taiwan, Malaysia and Thailand (the recent economic setbacks have not permanently punctured the economic bublies). Then there are 200 million more in Brazil, Argentina, Venezuela and Mexico, and more again in Hungary and other countries of Eastern Europe, also Turkey. Put them all together and they total about as many as the 800 million long established consumers in the ultra rich countries (the OECD grouping). When the current economic hiccups in Asia are left behind, the ranks of the new consumers can be expected to rise rapidly.

But they cannot hope to become super consumers. Where would all the extra gain come from? How could the global climate tolerate the huge additional pulse of carbon dioxide? There are all kinds of other environmental reasons to suppose that environmental constraints will become all the more constraining. True, technology could help moderate the environmental impac' We could enjoy twice as much material prosperity while using only half as much natural resources and causing half as much pollution and waste. But the new consumers will want to pursue the American dream to the hilt, and it is hard to see that the best technologies could enable huge numbers of affluent aspirants, perhaps two billion people by 2010, enjoying even half the material prosperity of Americans with average household incomes of $40,000.

But it is true "prosperity"—mental and emotional as well as material? Or is the American dream becoming a nightmare with its hurried lifestyles and declining leisure time, where the shopping mall is the ultimate mecca, and the good life is a case of piling up goodies?

In any case, we cannot expect the new consumers to forego their "rightful share" of affluence unless the long-time affluent agree to cut back on their environmental ruinous lifestyles. It is these communities that must offer a strong example, and soonest. Where is the political leader who will espouse the new vision, however much it may be perceived as the ultimate vote loser?

# 25 The Population Challenge

During the last half-century world population has more than doubled, climbing from 2.5 billion in 1950 to 5.9 billion in 1998. Those of us born before 1950 are members of the first generation to witness a doubling of world population. Stated otherwise, there has been more growth in pollution since 1950 than during the 4 million years since our early ancestors first stood upright.

This unprecedented surge in population combined with rising individual consumption, is pushing our claims on the planet beyond its natural limits. Water tables area falling on every continent as demand exceeds the sustainable yield of aquifers. Eventual aquifer depletion will bring irrigation cutbacks and shrinking harvests. Our growing appetite for seafood has pushed oceanic fisheries to their limits and beyond. Collapsing fisheries tell us we can go no further. The Earth's temperature is rising, promising changes in climate that we cannot even anticipate. We are triggering the greatest extinction of plant and animal species since the dinosaurs disappeared. As our numbers go up, their numbers go down.

These effects of population growth are relatively recent, but assertions that population growth could affect human welfare art not. In 1798 Thomas Malthus, a British clergyman and intellectual, warned in his famous piece, *An Essay on the Principles of Population,* of the tendency for population to grow exponentially while food supply grew arithmetically. He saw a world where human numbers would continually press against available food supplies.

During the 200 years since Malthus issued his warning, famine has visited countries as diverse as Ireland and India,

Ethiopia and China. Indeed, despite the near-tripling of the world grain harvest since 1950 the hungry and malnourished in 1998 number an estimated 840 million—nearly as many people as lived in the world when Malthus penned his essay.

But the nature of famine has changed. Whereas it was once geographically defined by areas of poor harvests, today famine is economically defined by low income in those segments of society that lack the purchasing power to buy enough food. Famine concentrated among the poor is less visible than the more traditional version but is no less real.

In addition to checks imposed by food shortages, there is evidence that other checks on population growth are now emerging, such as new infectious diseases, including AIDS, Ethnic conflicts within societies, such as Rwanada and the Sudan, are also taking a growing toll. Water shortages on a scale that would deprive people of enough water to produce food could undermine governments.

The evidence gathered here indicates that the rapid population growth prevailing in a majority of the world's countries is not going to continue much longer. Either countries will get their act together, shifting quickly to smaller families, or death rates will rise from one or more of the stresses just mentioned. As human demands press against more and more of the Earth's limits, the questions is not whether population growth will slow, but how. Will it be because countries do it humanely by shifting quickly to smaller families? Or because they fail to do so, and nature ruthlessly imposes its own constraints? In a world facing many challenges as it prepares to enter the next century, this may be the most challenging of all.

Estimates of future numbers are based on the latest United Nations population projections, using their medium level figures. Under this scenario, world population will grow from 6.1 billion in 2000 to 9.4 billion in 2050—a gain of 3.3 billion. The other two U.N. projections put global population in 2050 as high as 11.2 billion or as low as 7.7 billion. While the medium scenario is judged by the U.N. demographers as the one most likely to materialize, it is not an inevitable population path for the next century. Indeed, because the projections are based exclusively on demographic assumptions and do not take into account the environmental limits to carrying capacity, they should be viewed as a first pass rather than the final word on estimates of future population.

We use the medium-level projections to give an idea of the strain this "most likely" outcome would place on ecosystems and governments, and the urgent need to break from the business-as-usual scenario. The mid-level projected growth in population of 3.3 billion by 2050 is very close to the growth that will have occurred between 1950 and 2000, some 3.6 billion. But there is one difference. During the half-century now ending, the growth occurred in both industrial and developing countries. During the next half-century, the entire burden of the projected increase of 3.3 billion will be in developing countries, many of which are hard-pressed to satisfy even existing demands on resources. In fact, the population of the industrial world is expected to decline slightly.

The annual rate of world population growth reached its historical high in 1964 at 2.2 per cent. Since then, it has been slowly declining, dropping to 1.4 per cent in 1998. Despite the failing rate of growth the number of people aged each year increased from 72 million in 1964 to the all-time peak of 87 million in 1990. Since then the annual addition has also declined, falling to 80 million in 1997, where it is projected to remain for the next two decades before starting to decline.

The population projections for individual countries vary more widely than at any time in history. At mid-century populations were growing every where, but today they have stabilized in some 32 countries, while they continue to expand in some countries at 3 per cent or more a year, Indeed, the world can be divided demographically into two camps: countries that have achieved population stability or are well on the way to doing so, and those that have not.

With the exception of Japan, all the nations in the first camp are in Europe. And all re industrial countries. The populations of some countries, including Russia, Japan, and

Germany, are actually projected to decline some what over the next half-century. In addition to the 32 countries, containing 12 per cent of world population, that have stabilized their populations, in another 39 countries fertility has dropped to replacement level (roughly two children per couple) or below. Among the countries in this category are China and the United States the first and third largest countries, which together contain 26 per cent of the world's people.

Although fertility in these 39 countries has fallen below replacement level, their populations have not yet stabilized because there is a disproportionately large number of young people moving into the reproductive age group. Thus even if they hold their fertility at replacement level, population may continue to grow for several decades before it stabilizes. It was this realisation that led China nearly 20 years ago to shift its goal from a two-child to a one-child family. Leaders in Beijing realized that, if they did not do this they would be faced with adding the equivalent of another India to their population—a development they considered potentially disastrous for their people.

In contrast to this group some countries are projected to triple their populations over the next half-century. For example, Ethiopia's current population of 62 million will more than triple, as it climbs to 213 million in 2050. Pakistan's population is projected to go from 148 million to 357 million, surpassing that of the United States before 2050 today to 339 million, giving it more people in 2050 than there were in all of Africa in 1950. From an environmental vanage point, considering particularly the availability of water and cropland, it is unlikely that the projected population increases for these three countries, and other countries with similar projected gains, will materialise.

As hard as it is to imagine the addition of another 3.3 billion people to the world's population, it is even more difficult to understand the effects of adding such numbers. As we look back over the last half-century, we see that World lumber use more than doubled, paper use increased nearly sixfold, grain consumption nearly tripled, water use tripled, and fossil fuel burning increased some fourfold. The relative contribution of population growth and rising affluence to the growth in demand for various resources varies widely. With lumber use, most of the doubled use is accounted for by population growth. With paper, in contrast, rising affluence is primarily responsible for the growth in use.

One way to understand the consequences of future population growth is to contrast some of the key trend projected for the next half-century with those of the as one. For example, we have seen a new fivefold growth in the oceanic fish catch and a doubling in the supply available per person, but biologists now believe we nay have "hit the wall" in oceanic fisheries and that the oceans cannot sustain a catch any larger than today's. Thus people born today are likely to see the catch per person cut in half during their lifetimes.

Grainland per person has been shrinking since midcentury, but the drop projected for the next 50 years means the world will have less grainland per person than India has today. Future population growth is likely to reduce this key number in many societies to the point where they will no longer be enable to feed themselves. Countries such as Ethiopia, India, Nigeria, and Pakistan will see grainland per person shrink by 2050 to less than one tenth of a hectare (one forth of an acre) far smaller than a typical suburban building lot in the United States.

Given that at the amount of fresh water produced each year is essentially fixed by nature, the water available, per person has shrunk steadily as a result of population growth, leading to sever water shortages in some areas. Countries now experiencing these shortages include China and India, along with scores of smaller ones. As irrigation water is diverted to industrial and residential uses.

The challenge to governments presented by continuing rapid population growth is not limited to natural resources. It also includes education, housing, and jobs. During the last half-century the world has fallen further and further behind in creating jobs, leading to record levels of unemployment and under employment. Unfortunately over the next 50 years the number of entrants into the job market will be even greater. Few things threaten the political stability of a country as much as growing as growing ranks of unemployed young people.

As noted earlier, the U.N. population projections cited here are based on exclusively demographic assumptions, which are not related to the population carrying capacity of local eco systems. These projections are purely statistical, based on historical data on fertility, mortality, and average life span and assumptions about future trends.

Based on the analysis in it, I conclude that the medium projection of 9.4 billion people in 2050 which U.N. demographers consider to be the most problem is unlikely to materialize. Rather the world is more likely to follow a patch closer to the low population projection of 7.7 billion by mid-century.

What is less clear is whether we will move to the lower trajectory because countries with rapid pollution growth quickly shift to smaller families or because they fail to do so and the resulting inability to manage threats from disease, spreading hunger, or social disintegration leads to rising death rates.

# 26 Law and Social Justice

Law reform in the service of democracy must find ways of protecting the vulnerable. Legal reform and "good governance" have vaulted to the top of the development agenda. International financial institutions and influential donors continually stress the importance of the rule of law, a healthy regulatory environment and strong and consistent enforcement of rights to successful economic development. In the New World order, the state's role is to facilitate private activity rather than guarantee the welfare of its citizens.

But there is growing concern that market reforms and globalisation are connected to greater social stratification and economic inequality. What is often overlooked is that legal reform may enhance rather than alleviate this stratification and inequality.

It is important to see legal reform as a key part of a broader set of policy, legislative and institutional reforms which are designed to create not simply rule-and norm-based societies but particular types of market economies. There are no "free" markets; functioning markets depend upon a legal infrastructure and commitment to the rule of law. The growing interest in legal reform indicates nothing if not the widespread recognition of this fact.

## Tradeoffs Between Efficiency and Equity

Respecting the rule of law and protecting rights however does not mean that there is any one best set of laws, even in a market economy. Yet legal reform projects in developing and transitional countries have become inseparably associated with the idea of single, optimal path or model. Current projects emphasize strong protection for property rights, the consistent enforcement of contracts and, increasingly, financial sector regulation as the foundation of an investor-friendly legal infrastructure. At the same time, states in transition to markets have been discouraged from adopting or retaining "excessive" regulations. Including protective labour market policies that might impede growth and efficiency.

Market-oriented legal reforms can affect the fortunes of different groups in at least three different ways. The first is through the types of reforms that are implemented. Because legal reforms allocate rights and entitlements, because legal reforms allocate rights and entitlements, different rule structures may well benefit different groups in different ways. In some instances, there may be tradeoffs between efficiency and equity. Strong property right will protect owners and entrepreneurs but may contribute to the disadvantage of renters and works, environmental and consumer protection laws protect the public at large but impose costs on businesses.

Second, people can be affected by the absence of particular laws. Labour standards and laws authorizing collective bargaining, for example, have been crucial in industrialized societies. If they are weak or missing as they are in many developing countries, or if they are indefinitely postponed because priority is given to implementing laws and regulations which facilitate economic transactions, vast numbers of people can find themselves worse off than they need be in the market for labour. Particular groups may also be harmed. Women with care giving obligations are likely to be systematically disadvantaged and shut out of better work opportunities without market regulations which ensure that part of these costs are borne by others. This is especially likely where social programmes and subsidies are reduced or eliminated at the same time, as has occurred in many parts of the world.

## Open Debate

Finally, where legal reforms follows a "standard from" or are designed by experts from afar, a common experience in transitional states, the risk is that local history and priorities will be ignored or displaced and democratic control over decisions about basic social organisation is weakened. To avoid aggravating inequality and worsening the position of those who are frequently already vulnerable in the reform process, three conditions need to be met.

First, conflicts of interests—between workers and entrepreneurs, for exaple—as well as the necessary tradeoffs that legal reforms often entail should be acknowledged openly, rather than hidden behind the veil of efficiency. This will allow countries to debate more openly the political and distributive choices that legal reforms involve. Second, donor countries and international financial institutions need to rethink the position that state "intervention" is usually or necessarily the enemy of economic development. Third, developing states need much more space, indeed they should be actively encouraged, to accommodate distributive, equity and social concerns not only through social programmes and tranfers but through the processes of legal and regulatory reform as well. This would allow greater attention to labour market concerns and environmental protection as well as to poverty alleviation and gender, racial and ethnic equity.

# 27 The Future of Work

The advent of an 'intangible' economy does not mean the end of work. But it does mean the end of familiar routines and rhythms, of job security, of rigid hierarchies and career planning.

People are worried about the far-reaching transformation of the economy. Are we heading for "the end of work". Yes, we have reached the end of the road. We are no longer creating jobs in industry and automation is sure to reduce their number in the services sector. The quantity of work is thus inexorably bound to decrease.

This thesis may be popular, but it is also mistaken and harmful. History shows that technological innovation has always created jobs on a large scale. In no way is the current trend leading to "the end of work" Just the opposite; the new economy contains huge pools of new jobs which can more than make up for the inevitable loss of traditional jobs.

Dematerialisation—the shift away from material products—is revolutionizing all aspects of work—its nature, its organisation and its relationship with other activities. It function is no longer just the manufacture of physical objects but the handling of data, images and symbols, The content of jobs is becoming more abstract. Skilled workers need to know a lot more about mathematics than their fathers or grandfathers did. Even milking cows and manufacturing require more and more calculation, evaluation and control.

## Financial Markets that Never Sleep

The organisation as well as the product of wok is also becoming increasingly intangible. The unity of time, space and action which characterized work in the industrial economy has disintegrated. Work is no longer a regular eight-hours-a-day, five-days-a-week routine. New rhythms have appeard—the hectic pace of financial markets which never sleep, the ups-and-downs of life in show business and the uncertainties of "just-in-time" production where components are delivered a few moments before the final product is assembled.

The new jobs are quiting familiar workplaces such as factories, offices and warehouses. Telework is increasing. Europe's teleworkers may number 10 million by the year 2000, up from one million in 1994.

This upheaval of worktime and workspace is going hand in hand with a functional explosion. The range of skills and types of work is expanding all the time. In the United States, the number of job categories has risen from eighty in the 1940s to nearly 800 today. At the same time, trades are dying out faster and faster, especially in information technology where many jobs have a short life of only a few years. Jobs are becoming simultaneously more evanescent and more pervasive, more dissociated and more integrated. On the one hand, fragmentation in time and space seems to be more extensive than it was in the industrial economy. On the other, information technology is strengthening the links between different stages of work and creating an overall fluidity.

## Disparities in Productivity

The new forms of work are non-linear. When handling information, knowledge and feelings, there is no direct relationship between the amount of efforts and the final result. This makes of very wide disparities in productivity. In industry, the ratio of the performance of an average worker to that of a good one is no more than one to five. But in immaterial work, an excellent programmer can be a hundred times more productive than an average one.

Non-linear work means non-linear organisation. The notion of a rigid, formal hierarchy based on unchanging criteria no longer makes much sense. All that matters now is technical, scientific or artistic skill and the ability to establish a solid relationship with the customer. Functional hierarchy is replaced by "brainpower"—authority gravitates to those who create and control the new stock of intangible assets: data, brand image, technological know-how and human capital.

The new techniques for managing human resources are individualizing the assessment of performance. Two people doing the same job may have different salaries and different status. Automatic across-the-board pay rises are being dropped and replaced by bonuses linked to results. There are no sinecures in the new business enterprise, either for rank-and-file employees, supervisors or technicians—the supposed beneficiaries of the new knowledge economy.

Business leaders are no longer a protected species. The head of a big American firm is ten times more likely to be sacked for poor performance now than was the case twenty years ago. The notions of loyalty and of indissoluble links between a firm and its employees are losing their meaning.

The changing nature of work has led to a big increase in so-called non-typical jobs, including part-time, temporary and flexi-time work and short-term contracts. Almost all the jobs created in Europe between 1992 and 1996 were part-time. This trend worries many observers who see to as hidden under-employment or disguised unemployment. But they are overly pessimistic. The growth of non-typical jobs is the result of the convergence of several persistent developments.

## Where the New Jobs Are?

The shrinking number of jobs in traditional sectors of the economy seems to be a general and irreversible trend. In rich countries as a whole, the share of industrial jobs fell from 28 per cent in 1970 to 18 per cent in 1994. Meanwhile, the share of the services sector grew steadily. Four major new sources of jobs can be identified:

***Handling Information and Knowledge:*** Computer services, research and development, teaching and training account for 40 per cent of knowledge workers. These high-intensity knowledge activities comprised 43 per cent of all new jobs created in the

United States between 1990 and 1995, but only 28 per cent of total jobs.

***Information Technology:*** Here there is a shortage of personnel. Professional groups are sounding the alarm and calling on governments to help. In the European Union countries, the imbalance between supply and demand is such that half a million jobs are waiting to be filled.

***The Health Sector:*** The growth of high-intensity knowledge services in this field is related to increased life expectancy and the ageing of the population, and the demand for physical and psychological well-being is also steadily increasing. The growth of expenditure on health is persistent and widespread. For the OECD countries as a whole, this spending grew from 3.9 per cent of GDP in 1960 to 7.2 per cent in 1980 and 8.4 per cent in 1992.

***The Leisure Economy:*** This has triggered the expansion of cultural, sporting and leisure services. It ranges from amusement parks and rock concerts to cultural events such as opera and major art exhibitions. The products of the culture industries have become mass consumer items. Never before have people read so much, listened to so much classical music or visited so many museums. Information technology is also going to add to this vast range of consumer choice. In sourthern California and New York, the entertainment and multimedia professions are among the main sources of new jobs.

In the labour market, the increase in non-typical jobs is one of the ways in which employers are responding to the pressures of competition and adapting to a global economy which functions seven days a week, twenty-four hours a day. To cope with the new situation, firms are having to figure out how they can use their workers more efficiently and flexibly.

The growth of non-traditional jobs is also due to changing demand. Consumers want to be able to buy a very wide range of goods and services at the drop of a hat, or amuse themselves any time, anywhere. To meet this demand, shops and places of entertainment have to be open late at night and on Sundays. Technology encourages this trend: the virtual economy of the Internet never sleeps.

The widening range of types of work also reflects long-term demographic trends, especially the greater number of women workers and longer life expectancy. Some see non-typical jobs as a necessary evil, while others, especially women with children, welcome the change.

The divide between traditional kinds of work and the new jobs is no longer watertight. People are increasingly switching back and forth between the two categories. In the course of a lifetime, a person may change from full-time to part-time work, from an office job to home office and from the security of a big firm to the adventure of entrepreneurship.

Changes in the nature of work are also breaking down the rigid frontiers, which marked off the world of work. The traditionally distinct fields of work, education and leisure are now interwoven and coexist flexibly in a kind of triple helix of social life.

The emerging intangible and relational economy has a huge potential for growth because it is not bound by the constraints of material scarcity. However, the transition to the now economy is an open-ended process. The state has a key part to play in bringing it about. Governments can slow down the rate of change by making it more painful and more costly.

## Obstacles to Change

Pessimistic scenarios are still plausible, such as that of an economy which generates few new jobs and is polarized between a small elite and the rest of the population who are marginalized and lie in precarious conditions. There is a big risk that this scenario will come to pass because current laws and regulations, as well as widespread pessimistic ideas about work, are powerful obstacles to change. Optimistic scenarios require a wholesale reform of institutional structures and profound changes in behavior and attitudes. Such far-reaching changes often run into strong opposition from the social and political establishment and come up against the weight of psychological and social tradition. But the gamble of a new approach to work must be made if the transformation to the intangible economy is to succeed.

# 28 Population Growth and Housing

Over the past half-century, the world's housing stock has grown roughly in step with population. yet for more and more people worldwide, adequate and affordable housing remains beyond reach, driving some into substandard dwellings and slums and others onto the street. This situation stands to worsen, for the need for housing worldwide is projected to nearly double over the next 50 years.

Although industrial nations currently occupy a disproportionately large share of the world's households relative to their population, virtually all future growth will occur in developing countries, where housing requirements will more than double by the middle of the twenty-first century. This phenomenal growth results from the potent synergy between population growth and a shift toward fewer people per household—a trend that is especially pronounced where economic growth is rapid.

HABITAT, the United Nations Centre for Human Settlements, has projected housing requirements based on roughly a 30-per cent reduction in people per household over the next 50 years. These figures are purely statistical estimates and do not consider possible checks in housing growth, such as materials or financial constraints, intensified land competition, or increased poverty. Our own projections assume that household size will indeed decrease, as fertility rates drop and as extended families become more rare, but by a more modest 15 per cent.

Over the next 50 years, housing needs in Africa and the Middle East are expected to increase more than threefold, with tremendous gains in the region's most populous nations;

demands are to increase 3.5 times in Nigeria and 4.5 times in Ethiopia. Although less dramatic percentage increase are expected in Asia, the doubling of households in the region will require nearly 700 million additional homes by 2050. Still, some countries there, such as Pakistan and neighbouring Afghanistan, will see housing needs increase nearly three and a half times.

The projected growth in housing needs becomes all the more daunting given that rapid population growth—combined with rapid urban growth—has already left a large share of the world's population without adequate housing. HABITAT estimates that at least 600 million urban dwellers and more than 1 billion rural dwellers in Africa, Asia, and Latin America live in housing that is so overcrowded and of such poor quality with such inadequate provision for water, sanitation, drainage, and garbage collection that their lives and their health are continually at risk.

As the supply of housing falls behind demand, the quality of available housing tends to deteriorate. Cheaper, less durable materials, such as scrap metal and cardboard, are substituted for more expensive, weather-resistant materials, such as concrete and wood. Fierce competition in swelling urban areas for desirable land can eliminate all hope of low-income households acquiring plot for housing. As choice of location dwindles, shantytowns and other low-quality settlements develop on marginal land ill suited for housing-in floodplains, on steep hillsides, near garbage dumps or other environmentally risky sites. From New York to Beijing, cities are faced with land and materials constraints even as their populations continue to grow.

At the same time, housing area per person continues to increase in certain nationals and among the more affluent segments of other nations, placing additional stress on prime space and building materials. In the United States, Western Europe, and Japan—a nation traditionally known for small dwellings—floor space per person has more than doubled in new single family homes since mid-century. The global disparity in floor space per person—Washington, D.C., at the high end with 70 square meters per person, and most of humanity at around 9 square meters per person—will likely mimic the growing global disparity in income, as wealthy household scale up and poorer households fill up.

Housing can provide a connection to a supply of fresh water and sanitation facilities. But as its quality deteriorates, so do these basic amenities. Half the world's people are without access to sanitation and nearly this many—2.7 billion—are without a reliable source of safe drinking water. Shortage of housing that provides these basic services are most acute in cities, where rapid urbanisation and high population densities place heightened demands on infrastructure. And still housing needs are projected to soar in the regions of the world where access to water and sanitation are most constrained.

The ultimate manifestation of population growth outstripping the supply of housing is homelessness. The United Nations estimates that a least 100 million of the world's people—roughly the same as the population of Mexico have no home; the number tops 1 billion if those with especially insecure or temporary accommodations, such as squatters, are included. In many developing countries, squatter communities are home to 30-60 per cent of the urban population. There are some 250, 000 pavement dwellers in Bombay alone. Humans who are born, live, and die in the streets—are common in all major cities. Unless the world moves to a lower population trajectory, the ranks of homeless are likely to swell dramatically.

# 29 Population Growth and Jobs

Since mid-century, the world's labour force has more than doubled, from 1.2 billion people to 2.7 billion, outstripping the growth in job creation. As a result, the United Nations International Labour Organisation estimates that nearly 1 billion people, approximately 30 per cent of the global work force, are unemployed or underemployed (working but not earning enough to meet basic needs). Over the next half-century, the world will need to create more than 1.9 billion jobs—all of them in the developing world—just to maintain current levels of employment.

As economists often note, while population growth may boost labour demand (through economic activity and demand for goods), it will most definitely boost labour supply. During the next 50 years, almost 40 million people will enter the global labour force—defined as those between the ages of 15 and 65 seeking work-each year. Between 1995 and 2050, some 1.9 billion additional jobs will need to be created to absorb these new would-be workers. The most pressing needs will be found in the world's poorest nations—a sobering example of the vicious cycle linking poverty and population growth.

As the children of today represent the workers of tomorrow, the interaction between population growth and jobs is most acute in nations with young populations. Nations such as Peru, Mexico, Indonesia, and Zambia with more than half their population below the age of 25 will feel the burden of this labour flood. In the Middle East and Africa, 40 per cent of the population is under the age of 15. Since new entrants into the labour force were born at least 15 years ago, measures to reduce population growth have a delayed effect on the growth of the labour force, highlighting the urgency of taking action on population.

Nowhere is the employment challenge greater than in Africa, where at least 40 per cent of the population lives in absolute poverty. Although 8 million people entered the sub-Saharan work force in 1997, by 2030 this resource-scarce region will have to absorb more than 17 million new entrants each year. Over the next half-century, Nigeria's labour force is projected to grow by 246 per cent and Ethiopia's will soar by 337 per cent—both faster than growth of the general population. At current growth rates, the size of the labour force in sub-Saharan Africa will more than triple by 2050.

As a result of unprecedented population growth and increasing acceptance of female participation in the work force, the number of people seeking jobs in the Middle East and North Africa, a region already plagued by double-digit unemployment rates, will double in the next 50 years. In Algeria, where unemployment stands at 22 per cent, the labour force is growing at a staggering 4.2 per cent annually, and the number seeking work will more than double by 2050. Egypt alone will need to create 26 million more jobs by 2050 as its total population hits 115 million.

Nations throughout Asia will also see phenomenal increases in the numbers seeking work, including Pakistan, where the work force will grow from 70 million in 1998 to 205 million by 2050. Over the next 25 years, India will add nearly 10 million to its work force each year. During the same period, China will add nearly 6 million annually due to population growth alone, compounding the work shortages caused by the current flood of migrants to China's coastal cities and by massive layoffs—estimated at more than 30 million—as state-run operations are scaled back.

Nations are hard-pressed to educate and train rapidly growing numbers of young people in marketable skills for the global workplace. Moreover, meeting the basic needs of a growing population draws scarce foreign exchange and other resources from investments in education and job creation. Throughout the world, young people entering the work force are increasingly faced with unemployment and social marginalisation. In most societies, unemployment rates for those under 25 are substantially higher than for older people.

Surplus farmland once served as a traditional source of employment for growing populations, as new land could be plowed to generate work and income. However, global per capita Greenland has dropped by half and considerably more in certain nations since 1950. Moreover, the machanisation of agriculture fuels the exodus of job seekers into the world's urban areas, where unemployment is often most acute heavily reliant on natural capital in the past, future job creation will require massive amounts of financial capital to jump-start the industrial and service sectors.

As the balance between the demand and supply of labour is tipped by population growth, wages—the price of labour—tend to decreases. And in a situation of labour surplus, the quality of jobs may not improve as fast for workers will settle for longer hours, fewer benefits and less control over work activities.

Employment is the key to obtaining food, housing, health services, and education, in addition to providing self-respect and self-fulfilment. Rising numbers of unemployed people could drive global poverty and hunger to precarious levels, fueling political instability.

# Bibliography


Agarwal, Bina. 1992. "Gender Relations and Food Security: Coping with Seasonality, Drought and Famine in South Asia." In Lourdes Beneria and Shelley Feldman, Eds. *Unequal Burden: Economic Crises, Persistent Poverty, and Women' Work*. Boulder, Colo.: Westview Press.

Agarwal, Bina. 1997. "Bargaining and Gender Relations: Within and Beyond the Household." *Feminist Economics* 3(1): 1-51.

Akerlof, Geogre, A., and Rachel E. Kranton, 1999. *Economics and Identity*. Washington, D.C.: Brookings Institute.

Alkire, Sabina. 1999," Operationalizing Amartya Sen's Capability Approach to Human Development: A Framework for Identifying 'Valuable' Capabilites." Ph. D. diss, Oxford University.

Baulch, Bob. 1996a. "Neglected Trade-Offs in Poverty Measurement." *IDS Bulletin* 27(1): 36-42.

Baulch, Bob. 1996b. "The New Poverty Agenda: A Disputed Consensus." *IDS Bulletin* 27(1): 1-10.

Bebbington A., and T. Perreault. 1999. "Social Capital, Development and Access to Resources in Highland Ecuador." *Economic Geography* October.

Beneria, Lourdes, 1989. "Gender and the Global Economy." In Arthur MacEwan and William Tabb, Eds. *Instability and Change in the Global Economy*. New York: Monthly Review Press.

Berelson, Bernard. 1954. "Content Analysis," *Handbook of Social Psychology*. Vol. 1 Reading, Mass; Addision-Wesley.

Bhatt, Mihir. 1999. "Natural Disasters as National Shocks to the Poor and Development," Disaster Mitigation Institute, Ahmedabad, India.

Booth, David, Jeremy Holland, Jesko Hentschel, Peter Lanjouw, and Alicia Herbert. 1998. *Participation and Combined Methods in African Poverty Assessment:Renewing the Agenda*. Department for

International Development (DFID), U.K.: Social Development Division and Africa Division.

Bradley, Christine, 1994. "Why Male Violence Against Women is a Development Issue; Reflections from Papua New Guinea." In Miranda Davies, Ed. *Women and Violence: Realities and Responses, Worldwide.* London: Zed Books.

Brunetti, Aymo, Gregory Kisunko, and Beatrice Weder. 1997. "Institutions in Transition: Reliability of Rules and Economic Performance in Former Socialist Countries." Policy Research Working Paper 1809. Washington, D.C.: World Bank.

Carvalho, Soniya, and Howard White, 1997, "Combining the Quantitative and Qualitative Approaches to Poverty Measurement and Analysis: The Practice and the Potential." Technical Paper 366. Washington, D.C.: World Bank.

Castellas, Manuel. 1997. *The Power of Identity.* Malden, Mass.: Blackwell Publishers.

Cernea, Michael 1979, "Entry Points for Sociological Knowledge in the Project Cycle." Agricultural and Rural Development Department. Washington, D.C.: World Bank.

Cernea, Michael, Ed. 1985. *Putting People First.* New York: Oxford University Press.

Cernea, Micheal, with the Assistance of Apirl Adams. 1994. "Sociology Anthropology and Development: An Annotated Bibliography of World Bank Publications 1975-1993." Environmentally and Sustainable Development Studies and Monograph Series 3. Washington, D.C.: World Bank.

Cernea, Michael, and Ayse Kudat, 1997. "Social Assessments for Better Development: Case Studies in Russia and Central Asia." Environmentally Sustainable Development Studies and Monograph Series 16. Washington, D.C.: World Bank.

Chambers, Robert, 1989. "Editorial Introduction: Vulnerability, Coping and Policy." *IDS Bulletin* 20:1

Chambers, Robert. 1994. "The Origins and Practice of Participatory Rural Appraisal," *World Development* 22 (7). Wahington, D.C.: World Bank.

Chambers, Robert,. 1997. "Whose Reality Counts?: Putting the First Last." London: Intermediate Technology Publications.

Chambliss, William J. 1999.*Poweer, Politics, and Crime.* Boulder, Colo.: Westview Press.

Charmes, Jacques. 1998. "Informal Sector, Poverty and Gender: A Review of Empirical Evidence." Contributed Paper for *World Development Report 2000.* Washington , D.C.: World Bank. October.

Dahle, Cheryl. 1999. "Social Justice—Alan Khazei and Vanessa Kirsch." Fast Company, Issue 30, December 1999, www. fastcompany.com.

Dasgupta, Parthra, and Ismail Serageldin. 1999. *Social Capital: A Multifaceted Perspective, Washington,* D.C.: World Bank.

Davies, Miranda, Ed. 1994. *Women and Violence: Realities and Responses Worldwide.* London: Zed Books.

Dollar, David, and Roberta Gatti. 1995. "Gender Inequality, Income, and Growth: Are Good Times Good for Women?" Policy Research Report on Gender and Development, No. 1. Washington, D.C.: World Bank.

Economist Intelligence Unit. 1997. *Armenia Country Profile, 1996-97.* Lodon: The Economist Intelligence Unit, Ltd.

Edwards, Michael, and David Hulme, Eds. 1992. *Making a Difference: NGOs and Development in Changing World.* London Earthscan Publications

Edwards, Roberts, and Michael W. Foley. 1997. "Social Capital and the Political Economy of Our Discontent." *American Behaviour Scientist,* 40(5): 669-78.

Esman, Milton J., and Norman Uphoff, 1984. *Local Organisation: Intermediaries in Rural Development,* Ithaca, N.Y.: Cornell University

**Press**

Fajnqylber, Pablo, David Lederman, and Norman Loayza . 1998. *What Causes Violent Crime?* Office of the Chief Economist, Latin America and the Caribbean Region. Washington, D.C.: World Bank.

Floro, Maria Sagrario. 1995. " Economic Restructuring, Gender and the Allocation of Time." *World Development* 23: 1913-29, Washington, D.C.: World Bank.

Folbre, Nancy. 1991. "Women on Their Own: Global Patterns of Female Headship." In Rita S. Gallin, Anne Ferguson, and Janice Harper, Eds. *The Women and International Development Annual.* Vol. 4. Boulder, Colo.:Westview Press.

Foley, Michael W., and Robert Edwards. 1996. "The Paradox of Civil Society." *Journal of Democracy* 7 (3): 38-52.

Foster, James, and Amartya Sen. 1997. "On Economic Inequality After a Quarter Century." 2d Ed. Oxford: Clarendon Press.

Fox, Jonathan. 1993. *The Politics of Food in Mexico: State Power and Social Mobilisation.* Ithaca: Cornell University Press.

Galtung, Johan. 1994.*Human Rights in Another Key.* Cambridge, U.K.: Policy Press.

Gelles, Richard J., and Murray Straus. 1998. *Intimate Violence.* New York: Simon and Schuster.

Giddens, Anthony, 1984. *The Constitution of Society.* Oxford: Blackwell.

Goetz, Anne Marie. 1998. "Women in Politics and Gender Equity on Policy: South Africa and Uganda." *Review of African Political Economy* 76: 241-62.

Greeley, Martin, 1994 "Measurement of Poverty and Poverty of Measurement." *IDS Bulletin* 25 (2).

Grootaert, Christiaan. 1998. "Social Capital: The Missing Link?" Social Capital Initiative Working Paper No. 3. Social Development Family. Washington, D.C.: World Bank.

Grootaert, Christiaan. 1999. "Social Capital, Household Welfare, and Poverty in Indonesia." Policy Reseach Working Paper 2148. Social Development Family Washington, D.C.; World Bank.

Grootaerr, Christiaan, and Deepa Naryan. 1999. "Local Institutions, Poverty and Household Welfare in Bolivia." Social Development Family, Environmentally and Socially Sustainable Development Network, Washington, D.C.: World Bank.

Holland, Jeremy, and James Blackburn, Eds. 1998. *Whose Voice? Participatory Research and Policy Change.* London: Intermediate Technology Publications.

Hyden, Goran. 1997. "Civil Society, Social Capital, and Development: Dissection of a Complex Discourse." *Studies in "Comparative International Development* 32: 3-30.

Jackson, Cecile, 1996. "Rescuing Gender from the Poverty Trap" *World Development* 23: 489-504.

Jain, Devaki, 1996. "Panchayat Raj: Women Changing Governance." Gender in Development Programme. United Nations Development Programme, New York.

Kabeer, Naila. 1997. "Women, Wages and Intra-household Power Relations in Urban Bangladesh." *Development and Change* 28(2): 261-302.

Kabeer, Naila, and Ramya Subrahmanian. 1996. *Institutions, Relations and Outcomes: Framework and Tools for Gender-aware Planning.* University of Sussex; U.K.: Institute of Development Studies.

Kaufmann, Georgia. 1997. "Watching the Developers: A Partial Ethnography." In R.D. Grillo and R.L. Stirrat, Eds. *Discourses of Development; Anthropological Perspective.* Oxford: Berg Press.

Korten, David C. 1990. *Getting to the 21st Century: Voluntary Action and the Global Agenda.* West Hartford, Conn.: Kumarian Press.

Krishna, Anirudh, and Norman Uphoff. 1999. "Mapping and Measuring Social Capital: A Conceptual and Empirical Study of Collective Action for Conserving and Developing Watersheds in Rajasthan, India." Social Capital Initiative Working Paper No. 13. Washington, D.C.: World Bank.

Krishna, Anirudh, Norman Uphoff, and Milton J. Esman (Eds). 1997. *Reasons for Hope: Instructive Experiences in Rural Development.* West Hartford, Conn.; Kumarian Press.

Leach, Melissa, Robin Mearns, and Ian Scoones. 1997. *Community-Based Sustainable Development: Consensus or Conflict?* University of Sussex, U.K.: Institute of Development Studies.

Lipton, Michael, and Martin Ravallion. 1995. "Poverty and Policy." In Jere Richard Behrman and Thirukodikaval Nilakanta Srinivasan, Eds, *Handbook of Development Economics.* Vol. 3. Amsterdam: Elsevier Press.

MacEwen Scott, Alison. 1995. "Informal Sector or Female Sector? Gender Bias in Urban Labour Market Models." In Diane Elson, Ed., *Male Bias in the Development Process.* 2nd Ed. Mahchester, U.K: Manchdester University Press.

Marshall, Gordon. 1994. *The Concise Oxford Dictionary of Sociology* New York: Oxford University Press.

Max-Neef, Manfred. 1993. *Human Scale Development: Conception, Application, and Further Reflections.* London: Apex Press.

Milanovic, Branko. 1998. *Income, Inequality, and Poverty during the Transition from Planned to Market Economy.* Regional and Sectoral Studies. Washington, D.C.: World Bank.

Milimo, John T. 1995. "An Analysis of Qualitative information on Agriculture: from Beneficiary Assessments, Participatory Poverty Assessments and Other Studies, which used Qualitative Research Methods." Ministry of Agriculture, Food, and Fisheries. Lusaka, Zambia.

Moore, Mick, and James Putzel. "Thinking Strategically about Politics and Poverty." DS Working Paper 101, Univesity of Sussex, U.K: Institute of Development Studies.

Moser, Caroline, 1998. *The Asset-Vulnerability Framework: Reassessing Urban Poverty Reduction Strategies*. Washington, D.C.: World Bank.

Moser, Caroline, Annika Tornqvist, and Bernice van Bronkhorst. 1998. "Mainstreaming Gender and Development in the World Bank: Progress and Recommendation." Washington, D.C.: World Bank.

Narayan, Deepa, 1999. "Bonds and Bridges: Social Capital and Poverty." Policy Research Working Paper 2167. Policy Research Department. Washington, D.C.: World Bank.

Narayan, Deepa, and Katrinka Ebbe. 1997. "Design of Social Funds: Participation, Demand Orientation, and Local Organisational Capacity." Discussion Paper no. 375. Washington, D.C.: World Bank.

Narayan, Deepa, and Lant Pritchert. 1999. "Cents and Sociability: Household Income and Social Capital in Rural Tanzania." *Economic Development and Cultural Change* (47)4: 871-8.

Narayan, Deepa, and Lyra Srinivasan. 1994. *Participatory Development Tool Kit: Training Materials for Agencies and Communities*. Washington, D.C.: World Bank.

Narayan, Deepa, and Michael Cassidy. 1999. "A Dimensional Approach to Measuring Social Capital: Development and Validation of a Social Capital Inventory." Draft. Washington, D.C.: World Bank.

Narayan, Deepa, and Talat Shah. 2000. *Gender Inequity, Poverty, and Social Capital.* Policy Research Report on Gender Development, Working Paper Series, Washington, D.C.: World Bank.

North, Douglas. 1990. "Institutions and Their Consequences for Economic Perfomance." In Karen Schweers Cook and Margarer Levi, Eds. *The Limits of Rationality* Chicago, Ill.: University of Chicago.

Norton Andy, and Thomas Stephens. 1995. " Participation in Poverty Assessments." Social Development Papers 9. Washington, D.C.: World Bank.

Orbach, Susie. 1999. "Psycho-analysis and Social Policy." Seminar Paper Presented to the World Bank, Washington, D.C., April.

Patton, Michael Quinn. 1990. *Qualitaive Evaluation and Research Methods.* New Bury Park, Calif.: Sage Publications.

Portes, Alejandro. 1998. "Social Capital: Its Origins and Applications in Modern Sociology." Annual Review of Sociology 22: 1:24.

Pottier, Johan, 1997. "Towards and Ethnography of Participatory Appraisal and Research ." In R.D. Grillo and R.L. Stirrat, eds.

*Discourses of Devlopment: Athoropological Perspectives*. Oxford, U.K.: Berg Press.

Putnam, Robert, Robert Leonardi, and Raffaella Y. Nanetti. 1993. *Making Democracy Work: Civic Traditions in Modern Italy*. Princeton, N.J.: Princeton University Press.

Ravallion, Martin. 1995. "*China's Lagging Poor Areas.*" *American Economic Review, Papers and Procedures* 89. 301-5.

Ray, Raka, and Anna Kortweg. 1999. "Women's Movements in the Third World: Identity, Mobilisation and Autonomy." *Annual Review of Sociology* 25: 47-71

Rietbergen-Mc Cracken, Jennifer, and Deepa Narayan. 1998. "Participatory Tools and Techniques: A Resource Kit for Participation and Social Assessment." Social Policy and Resettlement Division, Environment Department. Washington, D.C.: World Bank.

Robb, Caroline. 1999. "Can the Poor Influence Poverty? Particaptory Poverty Assessments in the Developing World." Washington, D.C.: World Bank.

Rodrik, Dani. 1998. "Globalisation, Social Conflict and Economic Growth." *World Economy* 21 (1): 43-58.

Rupesinghe, Kumar, and Marcial Rubio. 1994. *The Culture of Violence*. New York: United Nations Unversity Press.

Salmen, Lawrence. 1987. *Listen to the People*. New York: Oxford University Press.

Salmen, Lawrence. 1995. "Participatory Poverty Assessment: Incroporating Poor People's Perspectives into Poverty Assessment Work." Social Development Paper No. 11. Washington, D.C.: World Bank.

Salmen, Lawrence. 1998. "Toward a Listening Bank: A Review of Best Practices and the Efficacy of Beneficiary Assessment." Social Development Paper No. 23. Washinton, D.C.: World Bank.

Sartori, Giovanni, 1997. "Understanding Pluralism." *Journal of Democracy* 8 (4):58-69.

Schuler, Sidney Ruth, Syed M. Hashemi, and Shamsul Huda Badal. 1998. "Men's Violence Against Women in Rural Bangladesh: Undermined or Exacerbated by Microcredit Programmes?" *Development in Practice* 8(2): 148-57.

Schwartz, S.H. 1994. "Are There Universal Aspects in the Structure and Contents of Human Values?" *Journal of Social Issue* 50 (4): 19-45.

Sen, Amartya K. 1981. *Poverty and Famines.* Oxford: Clarendon Press.

Sen, Amartya K. 1983. " Poor, Relatively Speaking." *Oxford Economic Papers* 35: 153-69. Reprinted in *Resources, Values and Development.*

Sen, Amartya K. 1984. "Rights and Capabilities." In Amartya K. Sen, Ed., *Resources, Values ad Development.* Oxford, U.K.: Blackwell.

Sen, Amartya K. 1985. "A Sociological Approach to the Measurement of Poverty: A Reply to Professor Peter Townsend." *Oxford Economic Papers 37: 669-76.*

Sen, Amartya K. 1992. *Inequality Reexamined.* Cambridge, Mass: Harvard University Press.

Sen, Amartya K. 1993. "Economic Regress: Concept and Features," *Proceedings of the World Bank Annual Coference on Development Economics,* 315-54.

Sen, Amartya K. 1997. *On Economic Inequality* 2nd Ed. Oxford: Clarendon Press.

Sen, Amartya K. 1999. *Development as Freedom.* New York: Knopf Press.

Shah, Shekhar. 1999. "Coping with National Disasters: the 1998 Floods in Bangladesh." Seminar Paper Presented in June to the World Bank, Washington, D.C.

Shapiro, Glibert, and John Markoff. 1997. " A Matter of Definition." In Carl W.Roberts, Ed., *Text Analysis for the Social Sciences.* Mahwah, N.J. Lawrence Erlbaum Associates.

Silverman, David. 1993. Interpreting Qualitative Data; Methods for Analyzing *Talk, Text and Interaction.* Thousand Oaks, Calif.: Sage Publications.

Srinivas, Smita. 1999. *Social Protection for Women Workers in the Informal Economy.* Draft. Washington, D.C.: World Bank and Geneva: International Labour Office.

Standing, Guy, 1999. "Global Feminisation Through Flexible Labour: A Theme Revisited." *World Development* 3 (27): 583-602.

Stone, P.J., D.C.Dunphy, M.S. Smith, and D.M. Ogilvie. 1966. *The General Inquirer: A compturre Approach to Content Analysis. Cambridge* MIT Press.

Strauss, Anselm L. 1987. *Qualitative Analysis for Social Scientists.* New York: Cambridge University Press.

Tarrow, Sidney. 1994. *Power in Movement; Social Movements, Collective Action and Politics.* Cambridge, U.K.: Cambridge University Press.

Tendler, Judith. 1997. *Good Government in the Tropics.* Baltimore, Md.: Johns Hopkins University Press.

Townsend, Peter. 1971. *The Concept of Poverty*. London: Heinemann Educational.

Tripp, Aili Mari. 1992. "The Impact of Crisis and Economic Reform on Women in Urban Tanzani." In Lourdes Beneria and Shelly Feldman, Eds. *Unequal Burden: Economic Crises, Persistent Poverty, and Women's Work,* Boulder, Colo.: Westview Press.

Uphoff, Norman, 1986. *Local Intitutional Development: an Analytical Sourcebook with Cases*. West Hartford, Conn.: Kumarian Press.

Uphoff, Norman, Milton J. Esman, and Anirudh Krishna. 1997. *Reasons for Success; Learning from Instructive Experiences in Rural Development.* West Hartord, Con.: Kumarian Press.

Visaria, Leela. 1999. "Violence Against Women in India: Evidence from Rural Gujarat." *In Domestic Violence in India: A Summary Report of Three Sutdies*. Washington, D.C.: International Center for Research on Women.

Weber, Robert Philip. 1990. Basic Content Analysis. 2nd Ed. Newbury Park, Calif.: Sage Publications.

WHO (World Health Organisation). 1997. *Violence Against Women.* Geneva.

Woolcock, Michael. 1998. "Social Capital and Economic Development: Toward a Theoretical Synthesis and Policy Framework." *Theory and Society* 27(2); 151-208.

Woolcock, Michael, and Deepa Narayan. 2000. " Social Capital: Implications for Development Theory, Research, and Policy." *World Bank Research Observer* 15 (2), Washington, D.C.: World Bank.

World Bank. 1996a. *From Plan to Market: World Development Report 1996.* Washington, D.C.

World Bank. 1996b. *Sourcebook on Participation*. Washington, D.C.

World Bank. 1997a. *Poverty Assessment: A Process Review*. Operations Evaluation Department Document 15881. Washington, D.C.

World Bank. 1997b. *World Development Report 1997: The State in a Changing World*. New York: Oxford University Press (for the World Bank).

World Bank. 1998. *World Development Indicators*. Washington, D.C.

World Bank. 1999. *World Development Indicators*. Washington, D.C.

World Bank. 2000. *Poverty Trends and Voices of the Poor*. Poverty Reduction Group. Washington, D.C.

Wratten, Ellen. 1995. "Conceptualizing Urban Poverty." *Environment and Urbanisation* 7: 11-36.

# Index

## I



## J



## L



## M



## N



## P

**R**